# Decision Points

# Decision Points →

Boolean Logic for Computer
Users and Beginning Online
Searchers

Janaye M. Houghton
and
Robert S. Houghton

1999
Libraries Unlimited, Inc.
Englewood, Colorado

Libraries Unlimited, Inc.
P.O. Box 6633
Englewood, CO 80155-6633
1-800-237-6124
www.lu.com


*Aquisitions Editor:* Susan C. Zernial
*Production Editor:* Felicity Tucker
*Copy Editor:* Brooke Graves
*Proofreader:* Cherie Rayburn
*Indexer:* Susan Olason
*Typesetter:* Michael Florman

**Library of Congress Cataloging-in-Publication Data**

Houghton, Janaye Matteson
    Decision points : Boolean logic for computer users and beginning online searchers / by Janaye M. Houghton, Robert S. Houghton.
    viii, 155 p. 22x28 cm.
    Includes index.
    ISBN 1-56308-672-7 (softbound)
    1. Electronic information resource searching.  2. Computer logic.
3. Algebra, Boolean.  I. Houghton, Robert S.  II. Title.
    ZA4460. H77  1999
    025.04--dc21
                                          98-53624
                                             CIP

# Contents

Introduction..........................................................................................................................vii

**Chapter 1—Decision Points** ..........................................................................................1
George Boole and Boolean Algebra..................................................................................1
It All Depends.....................................................................................................................2

**Chapter 2—It All Depends. On What? Exploring Conditions and Outcomes**..................5
If-Then Statements: Conditions Stated Affirmatively and Negatively ...........................8
NOT: Inversions (Opposite Outcomes) ........................................................................10
If-Then Logic—The Computer Way................................................................................12

**Chapter 3—Boolean Logic AND More** .........................................................................15
Boolean AND Logic and the Simple Series Circuit........................................................22
AND Logic As a Search Tool on a Computer Database..................................................25
Focus to Find.....................................................................................................................27
Syntax of Searching: Variations on Searching with AND..............................................30
Advanced Searching with AND .....................................................................................32

**Chapter 4—NAND Logic: Combining AND and NOT**.................................................35
NAND Logic Both Ways..................................................................................................38
Searching Databases with NAND Strategies .................................................................40

**Chapter 5—Your Choice: OR** ......................................................................................43
Boolean Logic: OR and the Parallel Circuit....................................................................47
OR Logic As a Search Tool on a Computerized Database .............................................50
AND Gets You Less, OR Gets You More! Comparing AND and OR Search Strategies.......51
Searching with Synonyms: Another Use for OR............................................................53
OR Logic Using Partial-Word Searching........................................................................55

**Chapter 6—NOR Logic: Combining OR and NOT**.......................................................57
Using NOR Logic with Affirmative and Negative Statements......................................57
Searching with OR and NOT ..........................................................................................58
Alternative Notations for NOR—Advanced ..................................................................63

**Chapter 7—Combining AND and OR Logic to Make One Big Decision**.......................67
More Examples of Combined AND and OR Logic..........................................................69
The Final Decision.............................................................................................................74

**Chapter 8—Knowledge in the Information Age**............................................................75
Why Hunt?.........................................................................................................................76
Who Does the Hunting?....................................................................................................76
Where Do I Hunt?..............................................................................................................76
When Do I Hunt?...............................................................................................................77
What Do I Hunt?................................................................................................................78
How Do I Hunt?.................................................................................................................78
References ..........................................................................................................................79

**Chapter 9—Person, Place, or Thing**.................................................................81
White-Page Postal Address and Telephone Numbers ....................................81
White-Page Email Addresses ..........................................................................82
Yellow-Page Example.......................................................................................82
Email Conferences ...........................................................................................83
Newsgroup Examples .......................................................................................83
Liszt Newsgroups .............................................................................................85
Mailing Lists or Listservs ................................................................................85

**Chapter 10—Person, Place, or Thing** .................................................................87
Introduction .......................................................................................................87
Physical Libraries ........................................................................................88
Where to Search............................................................................................88
How Do You Find Sets of Online Libraries Using the Same Search Software?............89
Books and Resources for K–12 .....................................................................90
City Libraries ................................................................................................90
Bookstores .....................................................................................................96
Elementary, Middle, and High School Libraries.........................................100
The Library of Congress................................................................................103

**Chapter 11—Person, Place, or Thing**..................................................................107
Virtual World Problems....................................................................................107
The Hunt Across the Web.................................................................................108
The Top Level of the Web: Commercial Publications ...................................109
Encyclopaedia Britannica.............................................................................109
Time-Warner's Pathfinder ............................................................................109
The Second Level of the Web: Professionally Reviewed Internet Sites ......110
Family Filter from Alta Vista........................................................................111
Family Sites: Family.com ..............................................................................114
Adding Filters ...............................................................................................116
The Third Level of the Web: Subject Catalogs or Directories .....................117
Subject Search Sites ......................................................................................120
The Base: Robots .............................................................................................120
Northern Lights.............................................................................................123
Automated Search Routines .........................................................................129
Final Decision Points .......................................................................................129
Serving Ideas ....................................................................................................130

Answer Key .......................................................................................................133
Table of Selected Boolean Features ................................................................145
Index ..................................................................................................................149
About the Authors ............................................................................................155

# Introduction

As time pushes our boat toward the shoreline of the twenty-first century, we can see huge waves of information and choices crashing on the rocks and sand ahead of us. When the rising wave of choices splashes over those who finally reach the beach, *Decision Points* shows us a way to sort through it all. It also gives explorers the tools they need as they move past the beach and reach far into the Internet forest beyond. This book is intended to help teachers of all disciplines, librarians, students, and learners of all ages who wish to make this effort.

The first step in benefiting from what this ocean of ideas brings ashore is to make effective decisions. In this book, making good decisions is assisted by a form of mathematics known as Boolean algebra, also called Boolean logic. This Boolean logic uses simple terms, such as AND, OR, and NOT, to aid in decision making. These simple terms, when combined, are powerful operators for solving everyday problems.

Boolean logic plays a wide range of roles. It has proven to be a superb tool for designing computers and the software that runs them and for designing a wide range of electronic devices. At their deeper levels, computers manage information by using Boolean logic to change sequences of closed and open electronic gates. *Decision Points* explores Boolean logic in a more broadly applicable way, though. This book shows that Boolean is a syntax of language for analytical thinking—a level of thinking that serves as a stepping-stone to other higher orders of thought such as comparison, inference, and evaluation. In this way Boolean thinking transforms itself into an excellent tool to aid in the making of a wide variety of decisions.

The time it takes for the amount of information in the world to double continues to shorten. Though this fact is astonishing, an even more astounding development is occurring: our access to information through improved information system designs increases even faster than the overall growth of data. Furthermore, this world of information does not merely grow; its contents continually change as information is added and removed. *Decision Points* also explores key choices in making the best use of the information processors that stretch from your desktop computer to the search engines of the global Internet.

Unfortunately, information-age learners have been known to go starving while walking along this shoreline of abundance. Our information hunter-gatherers too often return with empty nets or hunting bags full of scraps that are of little value. As early hunters had to create different plans to trap different kinds of game, so must those in the Information Age. As Stone-Age hunters had to chip away unwanted rock to make effective tools, so must information-age hunters learn to use Boolean tools to "chip" away information that is not useful. This chipping brings to light the points and edges we need to make our ideas effective.

Boolean logic can play a role at every level of these problem-solving processes. Have fun with the following examples and puzzles, and then put this useful logic to work every day in your decision making and information searching!

*Decision Points* presents a progression of ideas and activities defining Boolean logic, search terms, and search strategies. The concepts and explanations in chapters one through seven are designed to appeal to elementary through high school students who are introduced to the concepts of search logic for the first time. The examples given are common experiences to students in that age range. However, older students and adults new to this subject may enjoy the simplified, step-by-step progression of the first seven chapters as well.

Chapters eight through eleven are designed for upper elementary students who are avid online searchers and high school students, college students, and adults who are familiar with online searching in a general way and who wish to refine their understanding of search logic, search terms, and search strategies.

# Chapter 1

# Decision Points

Should you spend your allowance on model rockets or on baseball cards? Should you advertise for babysitting jobs? Should you invite everyone in your class to your party, or just your special friends? Should you go to the gym to exercise or stay home and read a book? Should you open your mail or do your budget on the computer?

These are examples of the kinds of decisions children, teenagers, and adults make every day. Any day can bring hundreds of decisions. Most decisions are small and have very little lasting effect. Others are big and have major consequences. But no matter how big or small a decision to be made is, an *informed* decision is the best way to go.

That is, before a decision is made, it is best to think about all of the possible conditions that exist and the possible outcomes of the decision. After gathering information to make a decision, each of us may arrive at a different conclusion. Yet no matter what the outcome, decisions can be made in certain ways that use patterns of logic. Somewhere in the process of gathering information, a *decision point* is reached.

*Decision Points* is a book that presents several themes. Boolean logic, as described later in this book, provides the framework for this development. First, everyday logic statements representing common situations are presented. These logic problems represent decisions that we commonly face. The readers are challenged to "solve" and dissect these statements and then are encouraged to create new ones. Second, simple explanations and diagrams show how electronics and computer chip technology can take similar information and place the *decision point* inside a computer. Third, Boolean logic is shown as a way to search databases in libraries and Web pages on the Internet. This logic, along with a set of search terms, will help students hunt for information more efficiently.

## George Boole and Boolean Algebra

Don't let the words "*Boolean Algebra*" scare you! It is all about a man and a system that revolutionized the way we do work. A mathematician named George Boole (1815–1864) invented, quite by accident, the basis of logic for our modern-day computers. In an attempt to create a new form of mathematics, Mr. Boole identified certain patterns of logic that were later found to be easily translated into an electronic language—essentially, a "switch-on/switch-off" pattern.

Today, using tiny electronic switching mechanisms inside the computer, "decisions" are made with lightning speed within the central processing unit (CPU). These decisions are based on whether a tiny switch is on or off at any given time.

Computer programmers follow prescribed sets of instructions to "teach" computers how to make decisions to carry out instructions. This is called *programming*. Programming is made possible by sets of instructions called *languages*. Many of these languages are made up of the logic building blocks identified by Mr. Boole more than 100 years ago, long before computers.

The building blocks that Mr. Boole identified are AND logic, OR logic, NOT logic, NAND logic, and NOR logic. Computer decisions are made from these patterns of logic. For the purposes of this book, we have also added If-Then logic, which is basic to the understanding of Mr. Boole's logic patterns.

Mr. Boole's logic concepts are being used today to search databases for information in our schools, libraries, and businesses and to search data systems on the Internet. So let's get started exploring these concepts and see what they have to offer us every day.

## It All Depends

Have you ever asked a friend or a teacher about something you would like to do in the future? Were you frustrated when you got the answer "It all depends"? As frustrating as it may seem at times, with any plan, event, or activity, certain *conditions* must exist before certain results can happen.

You probably can't remember, but you began learning this as a baby. You learned that if you cried, someone would comfort you. If you laughed, others would laugh and smile around you. You also learned that if you wanted to eat and you made sounds, someone would feed you. Later, as a toddler you learned:

> If I reach for the cup, someone will give it to me.
> If I crawl to the toy chest, I can get out a toy.
> If I potty on the toilet, I won't be uncomfortable in my diaper.

And because of these associations, you learned to talk, reach, crawl, and use the potty. By the time you reached kindergarten, you began learning associations such as:

> If I wait in line, I will get a cold drink from the water fountain.
> If I raise my hand, the teacher is likely to call on me.
> If I talk out of turn and interrupt, the teacher will ask me to wait my turn.
> If I bring a birthday treat from home, the teacher will allow me to share it with my friends.

Older students are involved in making other decisions for themselves, based on the associations they learned in the past. For example:

> If I earn the money, then I can buy a ticket to the rodeo.
> If I study my lab books, then I may do well on the test.
> If I attend all of the practices, then I may play at the basketball game.

You have learned that certain things must happen for an event to follow. As you saw, the *outcome* you desired (going to the rodeo, getting a good grade, playing on a team) depended on certain *conditions* coming first.

Notice the *condition* and the *outcome* for the following situations:

1.  You need to earn five dollars so you can buy a ticket to the movies.

    **Condition**                    **Outcome**
    *If* you earn $5.00,             *then* you can buy a movie ticket.

2.  You must improve your math grade to be on the B honor roll.

    **Condition**                    **Outcome**
    *If* you bring up your math grade,   *then* you can be on the B honor roll.

3.  You must volunteer 10 hours of time picking up trash along the highway for your club to win free T-shirts.

    **Condition**                    **Outcome**
    *If* you volunteer 10 hours picking up trash,   *then* your club will win free T-shirts.

# If-Then Statements: Condition-Outcome

Now try these on your own. Write them as *if-then* statements with the *condition* first and the *outcome* following. Use the preceding examples to get started. Remember to determine what must happen first and what outcome will result.

1.  You need to hike five more miles to earn your 50-Mile pin for Scouts.

    If _____, then _____.

2.  You need to give two more pints of blood to earn a one-gallon pin from the Red Cross.

    If _____, then _____.

3.  You need to drop .08 seconds off your 100-meter swim time to place in the competition.

    If _____, then _____.

4.  You need to improve your sight-reading score by 20 percent to take First Chair in the band.

    If _____, then _____.

5.  You need to raise your batting average by .05 to qualify for the All-Stars.

    If _____, then _____.

6.  You need to improve your grade point average by .5 to be included on the Honor Roll.

    If _____, then _____.

7.  You need to read four more 200-page books to join the Accelerated Readers party.

    If _____, then _____.

8.  You need to cut 250 words from your essay to submit it to the Water Conservation Essay contest.

    If _____, then _____.

# Chapter 2

⟹

# It All Depends. On What?
# Exploring Conditions and
# Outcomes

Remember the person who said to you, "It all depends"? Did you respond, "On what?" This question suggests that you need to look closely at the situation and identify what conditions will bring about the result you have in mind. Sometimes the conditions may not be identified for you, as in the following example.

For these situations, you must *imagine* what condition would precede the desired outcome. The condition is not stated in the situation statement. As you study the example, realize that different people will be able to think of various conditions that are appropriate to the same example.

Given the same situation statement, conditions may vary, but remember that the condition must be *essential* to the outcome. In other words, the condition is a *prerequisite* for the outcome; it is required. The outcome must be a direct contingency of the condition; that is, it must follow naturally.

**Example**:

You want to buy cotton candy at the pep rally.

**Possible conditions:**

If I can go to the pep rally, then I will buy cotton candy at the pep rally.
If I can find my wallet, then I will buy cotton candy at the pep rally.
If I get my allowance tonight, then I will buy cotton candy at the pep rally.

**Activity #2**

# Finding the Prerequisite Condition

Identify a possible prerequisite condition for the following if-then situations. Remember there is no one correct answer. Various creative responses are acceptable if the condition is essential to bring about the desired outcome.

1. You want to swim today.

   If _____, then I will swim today.

2. You want to win a trombone competition so you can play First Chair at the spring concert.

   If _____, then I will win First Chair.

3. You want to build more on your toothpick bridge project, but you are out of toothpicks.

   If _____, then I will finish my bridge.

4. You want to continue to subscribe to *Sports* magazine, but you have lost the address.

   If _____, then I will renew my subscription.

5. You want to play on the library's computer today.

   If _____, I will play on the computer at the library.

6. You want to play racquetball after school today, but you forgot to sign up for a racquetball court.

   If _____, I will play racquetball after school.

7. You want to be a library aide, but you need five hours of orientation.

   If _____, I can become a library aide.

8. You want to play in the recorder ensemble after school.

   If _____, I can play in the recorder ensemble.

From *Decision Points: Boolean Logic for Computer Users and Beginning Online Searchers.*
© 1999 Libraries Unlimited, Inc. (800) 237-6124

# Have It Your Way: Personalized If-Then Statements

*Activity #3*

So far you have worked with situation statements that reflect goals of a student who is about your age. Now it is time to learn to write a situation statement on your own. Start this activity by thinking about a need you have or a desire you have for something to happen. Think to yourself, "I would like to _____."

Let's try some. Write down the next five ideas that come to you.

1. I would like to _____.
2. I would like to _____.
3. I would like to _____.
4. I would like to _____.
5. I would like to _____.

Now you have five "situation starters"! Think now about what is preventing you from achieving each goal, or what you still need to do to achieve each goal. You might state, "I would like to try out for cheerleading, but my grades aren't good enough." Fill in the following statements, using the five goals you just identified. You will have five situation statements when you finish.

1. I would like to _____, but _____.
2. I would like to _____, but _____.
3. I would like to _____, but _____.
4. I would like to _____, but _____.
5. I would like to _____, but _____.

Now you can clarify your situation statements by making them if-then statements. When you know what has to be done to bring about a desired outcome, you can get to work and try to make it happen! For example, "If I bring my grades up to Bs, I can be on the cheerleading squad." Write your situation statements as if-then statements on the following lines.

1. If _____, then _____.
2. If _____, then _____.
3. If _____, then _____.
4. If _____, then _____.
5. If _____, then _____.

# If-Then Statements:
## Conditions Stated Affirmatively and Negatively

You have seen some simple situation statements and found the conditions on which the outcomes depend. You have even written some of your own. Each outcome you have seen and written so far represented a goal, event, or activity that was desired by the person stating the situation. Each condition was stated in the affirmative. That is, if something happened (*affirmation*), then the outcome could take place. Let's now look at possible conditions stated in the negative. Look for negative words such as *do not, don't, will not,* and *won't.*

### Situation #1:

You need to earn five dollars so you can buy a ticket to the movies.

| **Condition 1** (as previous) | **Outcome 1** |
| **Affirmative:** If I earn five dollars, | then I *will* buy a movie ticket. |
| **Condition 2** | **Outcome 2** |
| **Negative:** If I *do not* earn five dollars, | then I *will not* be able to buy a movie ticket. |

This situation has two possible conditions: an affirmative one (stated positively) and a negative one. Each condition yields a different outcome. Each outcome is possible, depending on the condition that comes before it. That's why **it all depends!**

# Affirmative and Negative If-Then Statements

*Activity #4*

Find the two possible conditions (affirmative and negative) and the two possible outcomes for the following situations. State and write them using if-then statements with the condition first, followed by the outcome. Circle the negative words in the if-then statements.

1.  You need to backpack five more miles so you can earn your 50-Mile pin from Scouts.

    **Condition 1** (affirmative)          **Outcome 1** (affirmative)

    If I _____, then I will _____.

    **Condition 2** (negative)            **Outcome 2** (negative)

    If I _____, then I will not _____.

2.  You need to read 12 more books to become a member of the One Hundred Book Club.

    Affirmative: _____.

    Negative: _____.

3.  You need to donate two more pints of blood to earn your Red Cross one-gallon pin.

    Affirmative: _____.

    Negative: _____.

4.  You need to drop three seconds off your 25-yard backstroke time to qualify for the fastest heat.

    Affirmative: _____.

    Negative: _____.

5.  You need to submit your Web page design by August 15 to be included in the online contest.

    Affirmative: _____.

    Negative: _____.

# NOT: Inversions (Opposite Outcomes)

To this point, our logic problems have led us to discovering conditions and predicting outcomes. If the condition was stated affirmatively, the outcome was positive. If the condition was stated negatively, the outcome was negative. Now consider an inversion of logic.

**Negative Condition**

If you *do not* turn in your assignment,
If you *do not* return your library book,
If you *do not* push the "secure" button,
If you *do not* take the theft sensor off
    the new shirt,

**Positive Outcome**

then you *will* receive an incomplete grade.
then you *will* be fined.
then the alarm *will* ring.

then the door alarm *will* sound.

Observe each of the preceding statements. The condition is stated in the negative (that is, things that will *not* happen), but the outcome tells of something that *will* happen. That is an *inversion*. The logic has been turned upside down! If one condition *does not* occur, the outcome *will* occur. The condition is *opposite* the response. In the language of electronics, this kind of logic is called *NOT logic*.

Notice that you can state the preceding examples in the opposite way. The logic is still NOT logic.

**Positive Condition**

If you turn in your assignment,
If you return your library book,
If you push the "secure" button,
If you take the theft sensor off the new shirt,

**Negative Outcome**

then you will not receive an incomplete grade.
then you will not be fined.
then the alarm will not ring.
then the door alarm will not sound.

# Putting NOT Logic to Work

**Activity #5**

You have learned that NOT logic is logic in which the outcome is stated in opposite terms from the conditions. That is, if the condition is stated negatively, the outcome will be stated positively. NOT logic is used frequently in electronic alarm systems. Think about and write opposite outcomes for the following conditions. In these examples, the conditions are stated negatively, so please state the outcomes *positively*.

1. If you do not close the door, then (what will happen?) _____.

2. If you do not close the window, then _____.

3. If a key is not used, then _____.

4. If the correct security code is not typed in, then _____.

5. If the bank card access number is not entered correctly,

   then _____.

For the next five examples, invert the language of the outcomes as you did before. Here the conditions are stated positively, so the outcomes should be stated *negatively*. (Think about alarm systems as you do these.)

6. If you close and lock all the doors, then _____.

7. If you close all the windows and lock them, then _____.

8. If you use the key properly, then _____.

9. If you type the security code in properly, then _____.

10. If the bank card access number is entered correctly,

   then _____.

You can see that examples 1 and 6, 2 and 7, 3 and 8, 4 and 9, and 5 and 10 mean basically the same thing. It is the *language* of the situation statement that has changed.

From *Decision Points: Boolean Logic for Computer Users and Beginning Online Searchers.*
© 1999 Libraries Unlimited, Inc. (800) 237-6124

## If-Then Logic—The Computer Way

As you worked with if-then statements, you probably began to see that there is a limitless number of situations that lend themselves to this kind of organized logic. Not only do we base our daily decisions on these kinds of assessments (What are the conditions? What are the possible outcomes?), but computer programmers also use If-Then logic. This example shows how a computer can be programmed to accept "conditions" and then determine an appropriate outcome. It's a game called *Guess the Number*. The game goes like this:

> The computer generates a random number between 1 and 100. Let's say it is 49, but the player of the computer game does not know the number. The player attempts to guess the number by typing in a guess. The computer then gives feedback about that guess. Certain computer languages allow the programmer to use the words *If-Then* in the programming code. Here are the assumptions that the computer has been programmed to act upon.

# Conditions and Outcome Statements

If the player enters any number between 1 and 48, then the computer will present, "Sorry, your number is too low" on the screen.

If the user enters a number between 50 and 100, then the screen will read, "Sorry, your number is too high."

If the user enters the number 49, then the computer will read, "You got it! Beginner's luck!"

In this example, how many different inputs are possible? (100) How many possible outcomes? (3)

As you have seen, If-Then logic helps to define situations and implies that conditions and events occur in a *sequence*. Then it clarifies the *order* of events in the sequence. Ordering is as important to a programmer who writes for a computer as it is to all of us who go about a daily routine. Remember, personal computers receive and execute orders in a sequence, even though the time it takes to do so may seem instantaneous. The central processing units in our home computers can do millions of operations or steps in a second, but most computers still take the instructions one step (condition) at a time.

Computers make decisions based on information they receive. Information given to a computer is called *input*. Computers can receive input from keyboards and sensor switches (on independent circuits) that are external to the computer. The following are some scenarios in which a computer could monitor information and make a decision about that input.

# Computer-Monitored Scenarios

If the moisture drops below a certain level in a vegetable flat, the computer will "decide" it is time to turn on the water sprinkler.

If the doors to the car are not closed tightly, then the computer chip will "decide" not to allow the ignition to start up.

If the smoke detector senses smoke, then the computer will "decide" to turn on the sprinkler system.

If the smoke detector on the third floor detects smoke, then the computer will "decide" to turn on only the sprinkler system on the third floor.

If the yard sensor determines that there is movement along the perimeter of the yard, then the computer will "decide" to turn on the flood lights.

## Activity #6

# What Decisions Will the Computer Make?

After conditions have been identified, the computer acts on its instructions and input. This is its *decision point.* The following if-then scenarios are real-life examples of how computers and circuits make decisions. Match up the outcomes (the decisions) that the computer will make given the following conditions.

### Conditions

_____ 1.   If a sensor indicates that 100 cars have entered the parking lot,

_____ 2.   If a sensor indicates that someone is standing in the entryway of an automatic door,

_____ 3.   If a sensor indicates that an airplane is descending at too sharp an angle,

_____ 4.   If a sensor indicates that the water temperature in an aquarium has dropped too low,

_____ 5.   If a sensor indicates that the water temperature in an aquarium has reached the proper level,

_____ 6.   If a sensor indicates that a window in a business has been broken,

### Outcomes

a.   then the circuit will keep the door open until the sensor indicates that the entryway is clear.

b.   then the computer will sound an alarm.

c.   then the computer will turn the water heater on.

d.   then the computer will engage the automatic pilot to correct the angle of descent.

e.   then the computer will turn the water heater off.

f.   then the computer will automatically shut the gate and flash "Lot Full."

# High-Voltage Vocabulary

Review the vocabulary you have learned so far by matching up these power-packed words with their definitions.

1.  Outcome _____

2.  IF _____

3.  Negative _____

4.  Positive _____

5.  THEN _____

6.  Condition _____

7.  Series _____

8.  Logic _____

    a.  a way of thinking

    b.  a result of conditions being processed

    c.  a word that precedes a possible condition

    d.  meaning "not," something that has not happened, or something that is undesirable

    e.  meaning one thing goes before another in a simple sequence

    f.  a state of things or an event that may occur

    g.  a word indicating that something will come next

    h.  meaning something has occurred, or something that has occurred had a desirable effect

# Chapter 3

# Boolean Logic AND More

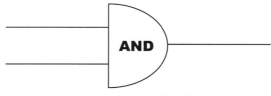

**Logic Symbol for "AND"**

You want to go to the movies Friday night, but you might have a late band practice. Even if you don't have band practice, you might not get your allowance until Saturday morning and you won't have the money to go. You have a problem! Or do you have two problems? Let's look at this logically!

**Condition**                                        **Outcome**

IF you are free on Friday night

     AND                              THEN You can go to the movies

IF you get your allowance on time

As you can see, before you can go to the movies, you need to solve two problems. Both conditions must be met before the outcome can occur. George Boole called this type of situation an AND-logic situation. That is, the first condition AND the second condition must be met before the outcome can happen. When more than one piece of information or two or more conditions are required to make a decision, you have an AND-logic situation. The following diagram shows the decision point:

IF

Free Friday night? yes or no

     AND                              THEN Can (or can't) go to the movies

Allowance on time? yes or no

Can you see that in this case both conditions must be met affirmatively—that is, with "yes" answers—for you to be able to go to the movies? Let's look at this in the form of a chart (see table 3.1). Read this chart down from each numbered column.

|  | IF | #1 | #2 | #3 | #4 |
|---|---|---|---|---|---|
|  | Free Friday night? | yes | yes | no | no |
| AND | Allowance on time? | yes | no | yes | no |
| THEN | Can go to the movies? | yes | no | no | no |

**Table 3.1**

Reading down column 1, you see that both conditions have been met (yes) so the outcome will happen (yes). For columns 2, 3, and 4, at least one condition is negative, so the outcome (going to the movies) will not happen.

Charts like this one are called *truth tables*. They are a way of looking at the logic of a situation in an orderly manner. The truth table can be oriented in a different direction for analysis, but the data remains the same. Read table 3.2 across.

| IF | AND | | THEN |
|---|---|---|---|
| #1 | yes | yes | yes |
| #2 | yes | no | no |
| #3 | no | yes | no |
| #4 | no | no | no |
| | Free Friday Night? | Allowance on time? | Can go to the movies? |

**Table 3.2**

Can you see how the symbol in figure 3.1 indicates two inputs and one output (result)?

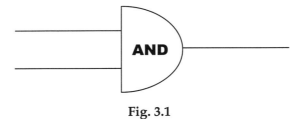

**Fig. 3.1**

## Here's another!

Your uncle calls and invites you to visit for the Fourth of July. You ask him if you can ride his Sea-Doo on the lake when you come. He tells you it depends! The Sea-Doo is in the repair shop and he hopes to have it out by then, but there are no guarantees.

You ask him if you can drive it by yourself this year. You tell him you are 12 now. He says he's not sure of the age requirement and that he will call the local boat safety patrol office to find out.

What pieces of information do you need before you can make the decision to ride?

Is the Sea-Doo repaired? yes or no
Can 12-year-olds legally drive a Sea-Doo? yes or no

These questions can be diagrammed as follows:

IF the Sea-Doo is repaired
AND                                    THEN You *may* drive the Sea-Doo
IF the law allows

When you arrive at your uncle's house, four possibilities exist. Look carefully at each condition and the resulting outcomes for these possibilities.

#1   The Sea-Doo is repaired
         AND                                    Do you get to drive the Sea-Doo?
     The legal age is 14 to drive it

#2   The Sea-Doo is repaired
         AND                                    Do you get to drive the Sea-Doo?
     The law says 12-year-olds can drive

#3   The Sea-Doo is not repaired
         AND                                    Do you get to drive the Sea-Doo?
     The law says 12-year-olds can drive

#4   The Sea-Doo is not repaired
         AND                                    Do you get to drive the Sea-Doo?
     The legal age is 14 to drive it

Consider these four possibilities. Only when *both* conditions are met (the repair of the Sea-Doo *and* the legal age of 12 for driving) will you be allowed to drive the Sea-Doo.

Let's put these conditions into a truth table to help clarify the conditions and outcomes. Read the columns in table 3.3 down.

| IF | Legal age is 12? | yes | no | yes | no |
|---|---|---|---|---|---|
| AND | Sea-Doo is repaired? | yes | yes | no | no |
| THEN | Allowed to drive it? | yes | no | no | no |

**Table 3.3**

Again you can see that only when *both* conditions are favorable will you be allowed to drive the Sea-Doo. This is an AND-logic situation as represented by the AND-logic symbol (fig. 3.2).

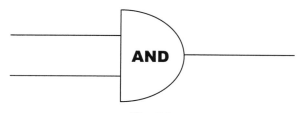

**Fig. 3.2**

Sometimes *more* than two conditions must be met before a decision can be made. Using the same example, let's add the following conditions.

#3   Must know how to swim
#4   Must wear a life jacket

Now we have four conditions that must be met before you will be allowed to drive the Sea-Doo. We can diagram them in this way (see also fig. 3.3):

IF
Sea-Doo is repaired
  AND
Legal age is 12 years old     THEN Will be allowed to drive Sea-Doo
  AND
Knows how to swim
  AND
Has and will wear life jacket

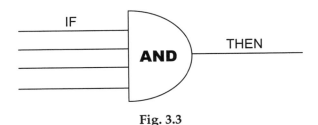

Fig. 3.3

Think about this AND logic. Could you add even more conditions? How many more conditions can you think of? Is there a limit to how many conditions you can have? You can probably see that the more conditions that must be met, the *less* likely it is that the outcome will occur. In this way, AND logic can be *exclusive*. That is, because all conditions are *required* to be met (because of AND), the more conditions there are, the more chance there is that one will not be met.

Notice how If-Then logic is important to AND logic. Once again, the statements of possible conditions (the preceding examples have more than one condition) are critical to the outcome. "If" defines what *must* happen, "AND" tells us *all that must happen,* and "Then" tells us what *will happen* as a result of "if" conditions being met.

Now, let's examine a nine-hole miniature golf course. Look for AND logic in the way the game is played. Golf is a game with a *series* of holes that must all be completed in a specific sequence to complete the game. That is, a golf game starts on hole 1 and *then* progresses to hole 2 *and* hole 3 *and* hole 4 and so forth. All the holes must be played before the game is completed. The diagram would be like this:

IF
 Hole 1_____
  AND
 Hole 2_____
  AND
 Hole 3_____
  AND
 Hole 4_____
  AND
 Hole 5_____

Hole 6_____
   AND
Hole 7_____
   AND
Hole 8_____
   AND
Hole 9_____
   THEN Golf game is complete

AND logic is all around you. Think about other games, contests, and sports that use AND logic. Let's look at the triathlon and the pentathlon sporting events and the Academic Decathlon.

**Triathlon:** In this competition, the participants must complete three (tri) separate sports activities.

IF
1. Complete swimming event
   AND               THEN Completes the triathlon
2. Complete biking event
   AND
3. Complete running event

**Pentathlon:** In this competition, the participants must complete five (pent) separate sports activities.

IF
1. Complete shooting event
   AND
2. Complete fencing event
   AND               THEN completes the pentathlon
3. Complete running event
   AND
4. Complete horseback riding event
   AND
5. Complete swimming event

**Academic Decathlon:** In this competition, the participants must complete 10 (dec) separate academic activities, accumulating points for each part of the contest.

IF
1. Pass mathematics test
   AND
2. Pass fine arts test
   AND
3. Pass language and literature test
   AND
4. Pass economics test
   AND
5. Pass science test
   AND
6. Pass social studies test
   AND
7. Pass United Nations test
   AND
8. Give an impromptu speech
   AND
9. Score well on a personal interview
   AND
10. Write an essay

THEN has completed the Academic Decathlon and is given an overall point score

# 10-Input AND Logic at NASA

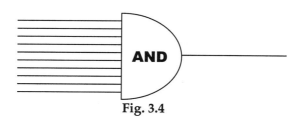

**Fig. 3.4**

If you have ever seen a picture of the National Aeronautics and Space Administration (NASA) mission control facility in Houston, you can form a mental picture of what a room full of computers looks like. Remember the film *Apollo 13* and the anxious moments in the control room while the computers yielded information about the bad news in space? With that in mind, design your own mission—but before blastoff, your computers must receive information that "all systems are go"! In other words, before the decision is made for blastoff, numerous conditions must be met (see fig. 3.4). Think creatively and list 10 conditions that must be met before you make the decision to blastoff! The first one is done for you.

IF

1. <u>The fuel tank is full</u>

   AND

2. _____

   AND

3. _____

   AND

4. _____

   AND

5. _____          THEN Blastoff!

   AND

6. _____

   AND

7. _____

   AND

8. _____

   AND

9. _____

   AND

10. _____

## Boolean AND Logic and the Simple Series Circuit

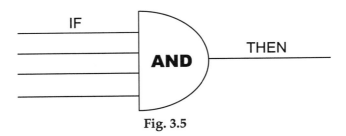

Fig. 3.5

We have pointed out that Boolean logic (see fig. 3.5) is used in computer circuitry and programming to make decisions. But how, given the complexity of the circuitry, can this be understood? The best way is to take a look at a simple circuit (fig. 3.6). There are two kinds, a series circuit and a parallel circuit. Let's begin by looking at the simple series circuit. (The parallel circuit is discussed later in this book.)

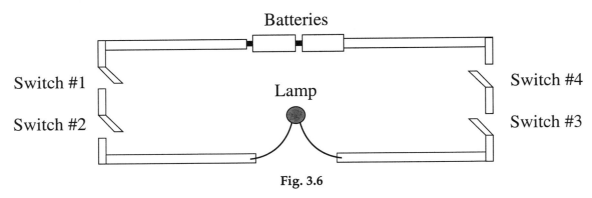

Fig. 3.6

You may remember this circuit layout from science textbooks and activities such as *Circuit Sense* (Janaye & Robert Houghton, Teacher Ideas Press, 1994). However, the simple circuits you have built may not have had four switches, but only one. Follow the path in figure 3.6 from the batteries around the design to find four open switches. Will the lamp be on when the switches are in this condition? No, the switches are open, the circuit is not complete, and the lamp will not light. Can you see how this circuit uses AND logic? In other words, all four conditions must be met (switches must be closed) to light the lamp. The conditions we have talked about throughout this book are called *inputs* when referring to electrical circuits. Therefore, using computer terms, this circuit has four *inputs*.

In a computer, each switch (input) may be controlled by a sensor or another circuit. That is, each switch will be either closed or open, depending on the information coming to it from a sensor (heat, light, moisture, etc.) or from another circuit within the computer.

Now let's close switch #1 (fig. 3.7). Will the light go on?

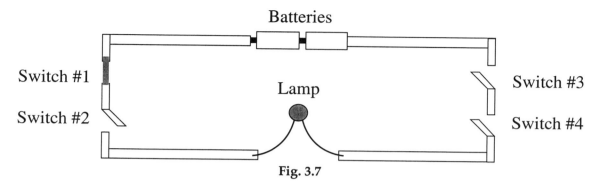

**Fig. 3.7**

No, three remaining switches are open and the circuit is not yet complete. This is a series circuit and *all* switches must be closed for the electrons to flow. Can you see how this circuit uses AND logic? In other words, all four conditions must be met (switches must be closed) to light the lamp.

Think about your electric clothes dryer as an example of a series circuit. Remember, you must close the door AND push a button to start the dryer. Neither one alone will turn it on.

IF
Close dryer door
AND                                          THEN dryer starts
Push "start" button

**Another example:**

Some automobiles come with the seat belts wired to the ignition. That is, if the driver's-side seat belt is not fastened, then the ignition will not turn on. Do you see the If-Then logic in the previous statement? Here is how the AND logic circuit works for this situation:

IF
Seat belt fastened                           THEN car will start
AND
Ignition switched on

*Activity #9*

# Making a Truth Table for a Four-Input Simple Series Circuit

Using the diagram of the simple series circuit in figure 3.8, make a truth table for a four-input simple series circuit. How many possibilities are there?

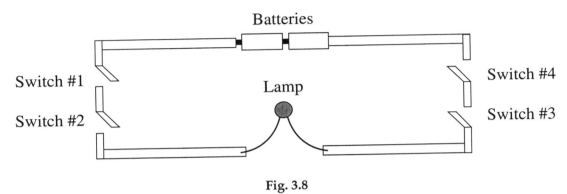

Batteries

Switch #1

Switch #2

Lamp

Switch #4

Switch #3

**Fig. 3.8**

Use your imagination to see different possible settings of the switches in the picture above. If you imagine that the switch setting is closed (the wires touch), then enter a plus (+) sign in the table below. If the switch setting is open, enter a minus (-) sign.

The first two are done for you. Read table 3.4 down the columns.

|  | IF | IF | IF | IF | IF | IF | IF | IF | IF | IF | IF | IF | IF | IF | IF | IF |
|---|---|---|---|---|---|---|---|---|---|---|---|---|---|---|---|---|
| Switch #1 | - | - | | | | | | | | | | | | | | |
| Switch #2 | - | - | | | | | | | | | | | | | | |
| Switch #3 | - | - | | | | | | | | | | | | | | |
| Switch #4 | - | + | | | | | | | | | | | | | | |
|  | | | | | | | | | | | | | | | | THEN |
| Lamp light? | no | no | | | | | | | | | | | | | | |

**Table 3.4**

# AND Logic As a Search Tool on a Computer Database

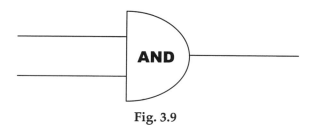

**Fig. 3.9**

Besides being a logic for everyday experiences, computer circuit design, and programming elements, AND logic (fig. 3.9) has yet another use that is essential to today's lifestyle. It is an *identifier* (sometimes called an *operator*) for searching the computer databases that are common in school and public libraries and available through the Internet.

These databases are also known as *electronic catalogs.* For many libraries, the online catalog has made the paper catalog obsolete. These catalogs are sets of words that describe materials, including books, articles, journals, reference material, indices of places and people, and more. You may search a database of information to pull out desired references to answer a question, solve a problem, or just provide an interesting pastime. No matter what your purpose, the search can be made highly successful and efficient by using Boolean search terms (logic concepts) to focus on and find information. Without these Boolean operators, searching can be overwhelming, time-consuming, and frustrating. The more you know about Boolean searching, the more interesting and productive your searching experiences will be.

Let's suppose the librarian has the books in the library entered on a database that is available to students by computer access. Let's suppose further that you are going to write a report about the most popular kinds of cats and dogs that people keep as pets.

When you go to the computer database, it will ask you what keyword or keywords you want to enter. Suppose you enter "cats and dogs." Then you watch as the computer tells you it has found five books that match your keywords (cats and dogs). Surely, you think, there are more than five books in the whole library that talk about cats and dogs. So you try again. This time you type in "cats" as a keyword. Instantly you see that the computer has located 62 books about cats. Then you type in "dogs" as a keyword and the computer identifies 78 books about dogs.

Now that you have identified 140 books about cats and dogs, where will you start? Maybe those first five books that were identified about cats and dogs would be the best place to start, as five is a more manageable number of books to look through than 140.

But why did you get only five books about cats and dogs? It seems at first glance that "cats and dogs" should give you more matches than "cats" only. The answer is that you used an AND statement in your search phrase. Because you called for "cats AND dogs," you got only those books that include *both* topics—and as you found out, far fewer books include both cats AND dogs. There were many more books about just cats or just dogs.

Using an AND-logic phrase *excluded* 135 books from the possible list. This may be a good thing. For your report, it would have been impractical and unmanageable to review that number of books. But how did those 135 books get excluded? Remember the work you did with conditions? By entering "cats AND dogs," you gave the computer two conditions that had to be met. This removed numerous books that did not meet those conditions and saved you time by listing fewer books to read.

# Searching with AND

Here are some search topics. Identify which topic from each set of two would probably find ("call up") the most and fewest references (called *hits*) on a database search.

1.  swimmers
2.  swimmers AND gold medalists
3.  dogs
4.  dogs AND sleds
5.  Boy Scouts
6.  Boy Scouts AND Eagle awards
7.  playwrights
8.  American AND playwrights
9.  musicals
10. Broadway AND musicals
11. Heisman trophies AND football
12. football

Now think of some of your own!

13. _____
14. _____ AND _____

Ask your teacher if you may try these descriptors on a database at your school or at your community library.

From *Decision Points: Boolean Logic for Computer Users and Beginning Online Searchers.*
© 1999 Libraries Unlimited, Inc. (800) 237-6124

# Focus to Find

You have seen how searching a database with an AND operator can be helpful by excluding unwanted information and presenting only references that include all of the keywords.

Another way to exclude unwanted material uses the concept of "focus to find." One common mistake a beginning researcher makes is writing to a topic that is too broad. Teachers guide students to narrow or focus a topic to be manageable and more easily covered. But, just as you saw earlier in this book, a starting point is needed. That is, a student may begin by saying, "I want to report on something about space." A statement or question can always be used as a springboard for future decisions.

With that in mind, one can see that a topic about space is much broader than the topic of "solar system." Solar system is, of course, a much broader topic than "planets." And "Saturn" is a less broad topic than all of these. Would a search for the keywords "solar system" yield information about Saturn as well? The answer is yes, probably, but it would be only one small piece of a much larger body of information. But a search using the keyword "Saturn" would yield focused, highly relevant information about Saturn. As you can see, narrowing a topic from "space" to the solar system, to planets, to Saturn is one way of *focusing to find* specific information in more manageable amounts.

By using both the "focus to find" technique and the Boolean operator AND when searching a database, you can call up highly specific information and save review time. To show how this works, let's explore the topic of Saturn more closely. We can ask: "Is this topic still too broad? What other keywords could be relevant to Saturn?"

atmosphere

weather

orbit

explorations

founding

statistics

temperature

Now we are ready to search. Using the keyword "Saturn," you would probably call up information about all of the preceding descriptors. But by using AND, a Boolean operator, you can continue to focus your topic. Try "Saturn AND atmosphere," for example. If that is your area of interest, this useful AND operator has already kept you from readings that do not address atmosphere on Saturn. Can you see how research and library time are saved when a powerful operator such as AND is put to work?

Depending on the database or Web site you are searching, you may not be limited to only two keywords. You may be able to further focus your search by including "Saturn AND atmosphere AND temperature." You can see that any match found as a result of this search would include all three terms.

The Boolean operator AND is a powerful search tool. As you have seen in examples of our daily lives, the concept of AND seems simple. But when it is put to work clarifying situations, defining conditions, and saving us work by focusing our pursuits on relevant information, the small word AND has a large influence.

Narrowing a topic for searching can be done by filling in a flowchart with increasingly more specific information. Figure 3.10 is an example of how to "focus to find" information and then use the Boolean operator AND to further define a search term. Notice that at each step a decision of direction must be made. Each step is a decision point.

Beginning statement: "I'd like to report on something on 'space.' "

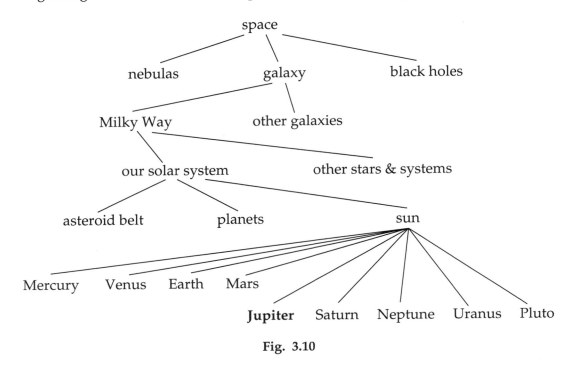

**Fig. 3.10**

Now that the choice has been narrowed to one planet, Jupiter, use Boolean AND to specify even further.

Possible search strategies:

1. Jupiter AND weather

2. Jupiter AND exploration

3. Jupiter AND exploration AND atmosphere

# Activity #11

# Narrowing a Topic for a Search

Here is an incomplete sketch of a flowchart to aid in decision making when choosing a topic for a search. Fill in the blanks by following the guide words. Add four more American presidents to the first set of lines. On the next line add one more descriptor. For the three suggested strategies, choose a president AND a descriptor.

## Presidents

American Presidents                    Foreign Presidents

_____ _____ Madison _____ _____

_____, term, politics, biography, influence


Possible search strategies:

1. _____ AND _____

2. _____ AND _____

3. _____ AND _____

Now choose a topic on your own and make your own flowchart. You will find that almost any topic you choose will be broad enough to break down into more focused topics. Here are some topics to help get you started: weather, submarines, Revolutionary War, inventions. Focus your topic with more specific terms as you move down the flowchart.

# Syntax of Searching: Variations on Searching with AND

As you become a more experienced searcher, you will find that although the Boolean logic concept of AND remains the same, different search engines or sites may vary in how they use the concept. The set of rules about how to enter the exact order of keywords, operators, and additional symbols needed is called *syntax*. *Syntax* is a word used to describe rules about word order in languages. For example, one would not likely say in English, "He has eyes blue," but rather, "He has blue eyes." The rules of English syntax require an adjective (color word) to precede the noun (eyes) that it is describing. However, syntax rules vary among languages. In Spanish one would say, "El tiene ojos azules," or, translated word for word, "He has eyes blue." The Spanish rules of syntax differ from the English ones, as this example shows.

Rules of syntax, or the processes by which to search specific databases, vary as well. It could be said that each database, although having Boolean search concepts in common with others, has a language all its own. To use any one database, you must learn the rules.

So far we have suggested defining a search by:

1.  proposing a question or statement

2.  focusing to find a keyword(s)

3.  using a Boolean operator along with the keywords to further focus the topic

We proposed using **Saturn AND atmosphere,** for example. One variation you may encounter is use of the + sign, which represents "must." This concept is the same as AND in the following search statement. It would be entered as follows:

+Saturn + atmosphere

This entry is interpreted to mean "any citation **must have** Saturn and **must have** atmosphere." In this case the + sign takes the place of the written word AND, but it does the same job. Yet another search engine allows a shorthand notation, so the searcher can enter:

Saturn & atmosphere

The "&" stands for AND and serves the same function.

Another variation you may encounter is the database's ability to recognize word order in its searches. That is called a *phrase search*. For example, to search for "electric eel" you may enter:

electric AND eel

You would get articles that use the word *electric* and the word *eel* in their texts. An option that is sometimes available is to put the phrase "electric eel" in quotation marks, as written in this sentence. This technique tells the search engine to keep the syntax the same as presented. That is, it is being directed to match only material that contains the words "electric eel" in that exact order. As you can see, this search would yield very different information. Complete the following activity page to learn how very different the results of these two searches would look.

# (Advanced)
# "electric eel" or
# electric AND eel?

Using the keywords **electric** and **eel** and the Boolean operator AND, identify which keyword search might yield which results. These are actual results from a database search with a well-known search engine. Place the number of the search that could have yielded that result in the blank before the result. Remember, words in quotation marks must be found in that exact order.

Search #1: electric AND eel _____   Search #2: "electric eel" _____

_____ a.   visit Aaron's dive shop to see a picture of an electric eel at this electronic address

_____ b.   Australian eel farms are electrically monitored

_____ c.   cabins on the Eel river with no electric hook-up

_____ d.   a British rock group named the "Electric Eels"

_____ e.   cooking curried eel on an electric stove

_____ f.   electric eels are being used to kill pain

_____ g.   "The Eel" (author, Unagi) is an electric story

_____ h.   place an order for an eel, using an electric order form

_____ i.   generating electric current on the Eel River

_____ j.   electric shock being used to stun unwanted eels that have invaded an unnatural habitat

_____ k.   watching the Eels play soccer created an electric atmosphere

_____ l.   the Eels ball club playing a night game under electric lights

*From Decision Points: Boolean Logic for Computer Users and Beginning Online Searchers.*
© 1999 Libraries Unlimited, Inc. (800) 237-6124

Did you find in Activity #12 that nine of the 12 references identified were not about electric eels at all? The importance of how keywords are used and the proper use of syntax (in this case the use of quotation marks before and after the keyword string) is obvious from this example. When doing the actual search on one large database, 468 matches to "electric eels" were found. When searching for **electric AND eels**, 355,165 matches were found. A smaller database found 12 articles on "electric eels" and 488 items on **electric AND eel**. One attempt to cut out unwanted articles about ball clubs and rivers is as follows:

electric AND eels AND fish

At first it would seem that adding "fish" would eliminate ball clubs and so forth. One database did yield fewer articles. However (depending on which search engine is used), most search engines just add to the three-part AND statement and create a prioritized list of hits. The items listed first include all three terms. Those that include any two come next. Finally, those that list any one of the terms are given.

It is important to understand how each search engine operates. This information is often placed on the opening page under a phrase such as "search tips," "guide to searching," "how to form a query," "help," or "how to do an advanced search." By accessing these search rules, you can learn how Boolean logic is used and the exact syntax required to get the most from your search.

## Advanced Searching with AND

An important reason to learn advanced searching strategies is so that you can pinpoint specific information and discard irrelevant and unhelpful information along the way. As you have seen, Boolean AND is extremely useful. There is at least one other search technique that can be seen as related to Boolean AND. One form of advanced searching with AND is a *pipe search*, so called for the insertion of a | between its terms. Remember, when narrowing a topic, we began with the large concept of "space" and then narrowed it slowly, one decision at a time. A pipe search does much the same thing after the searcher has done the thinking about focusing the topic. Here's an example:

sports | Miami | Dolphins

In this search, the computer first identifies "sports" articles, which, of course, will include a very large number of hits. Then, from that group of matches, the search engine searches for "Miami" and pulls out only those articles or sites that contain both "sports" and "Miami." Then the search engine takes those articles and searches for "Dolphins" within those articles. In this way an AND search has been accomplished. Each item identified will have all three descriptive terms.

But why not simply search **Miami AND Dolphins**? Because a search with these descriptors might give you the Dolphin Hotel in Miami, a dolphin research center in Miami, and the Miami Dolphin miniature wax museum in Peoria. But by using "sports" as a general concept and searching within that category, only sports-related articles will be cited. An actual search brought up 189 citations that included all three keywords. Compare that to the 9,573 matches when **Miami AND Dolphins** was searched!

Just as a simple circuit can have numerous inputs, a pipe search can have numerous "layers" of searching. The data from the preceding search is narrowed even further, yielding only 70 matches, when the following is used:

sports | Miami | Dolphins | 1997

Using **sports|Miami|Dolphins|1997|coach** yields only six matches. Remember that in a pipe search each succeeding search looks through only the previously cited items. Thus, all six resulting citations had all five descriptors in each article.

# (Advanced) A Variation on AND: Using a Pipe Search

Given the following starter searches, design a pipe search to find:

1.  *The Little Mermaid*     <u>movie</u>|<u>Disney</u>|_____

2.  *Independence Day*     _____|_____|_____

3.  *Apollo 13*     _____|_____|_____

4.  *Speed*     _____|_____|_____

5.  *Seven Years in Tibet*     _____|_____|_____

For each search, write possible unwanted responses that probably would have been found if the search had not been modified by using a pipe search.

Example:

1. mermaids, legends about mermaids, myths, songs of mermaids, etc.


2.


3.


4.


5.

# Chapter 4
# NAND Logic: Combining AND and NOT

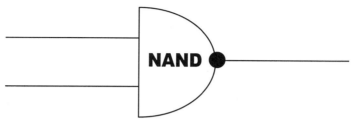

**Fig. 4.A. Logic symbol for "NAND"**

When a positive AND situation (in which two or more things happen) is joined with a negative conclusion (something will *not* happen), the logic is called NAND (NOT-AND). That is a combination of AND conditions with a NOT outcome.

Suppose you need a ride to your friend's house. Your big brother says he'll take you, so you get in the car and close your door. When your brother gets in the driver's seat, you hear a bell sounding and it doesn't stop. You ask, "Gerry, why is that bell ringing?" He doesn't answer, but he closes his door and latches his seat belt tightly. The bell sound stops! This is a NAND situation.

Can you identify the NAND logic here? What two things did Gerry do when he got in the car? He closed his door *and* fastened his seat belt and *then* the ringing stopped. What are the conditions and the outcome of this situation?

| Conditions (positive) | Outcome (negative) |
|---|---|
| Closing the door | |
| AND | Bell *stops* ringing |
| Fastening seat belt | |

Now imagine that you have a home security system that you turn on when you go inside. When you lock all the doors and close all the windows, the alarm will not sound. If someone opens a window or door, the alarm will sound to warn you. Let's look at the NAND logic here.

| Conditions (positive) | Outcome (negative) |
|---|---|
| All windows are closed | |
| AND | Alarm will *not* sound |
| All doors are closed | |

As you can see from these examples, this type of logic is commonly used in alarm systems. Can you think of other NAND logic examples?

Let's look at a truth table for the last example (table 4.1).

| IF | | | | |
|---|---|---|---|---|
| All windows closed? | yes | no | yes | no |
| AND | | | | |
| All doors closed? | yes | yes | no | no |
| THEN | | | | |
| Alarm sounding? | no | yes | yes | yes |

**Table 4.1**

Now let's compare this to the previously discussed AND situation about going to the movies on Friday evening. Remember there were two conditions to that AND situation as well:

1. Free Friday evening? yes or no

2. Get allowance on time? yes or no

As you look back over the truth table for that situation (table 3.1), you will see that three of the four outcomes were negative. That is, in three of the four possible outcomes, you would not be going to the movies. Now look again at the alarm system example (table 4.1). Notice that because the results are opposite of the input, three of the four situations are positive (for the alarm sounding).

When designing NAND logic, one has to be careful with the wording of the conditions and the outcomes. When using words like "raining" and "disqualified" or "awarded a traffic citation" in the expression, one has to take into account the fact that these words are already weighted with negative meaning for most people. For example, is it a positive or a negative thing to "not be disqualified"? Look carefully: the word *not* was in the expression, which might lead one to think that the overall impact would be negative. Technically, it *is* a negation. However, it might be the desirable result!

Remember the rule you learned in English class?

> Double negatives make a positive statement.

How about in mathematics class?

> Multiply a negative number by a negative number and you will get a positive number.

# Double Negatives: Are You Positive?

For the following examples, determine whether the overall effect of the statement would be a positive (desirable) outcome or a negative (not desirable) outcome for most people. Indicate your answer by circling the word that represents your thoughts. Positive is indicated with a "+" and negative is indicated with a "-". There is no need to fill in the dotted lines in these examples, but you may if you wish.

1.  If ........................, you will *not* be disqualified. + or -

2.  If ........................, you will *not* be awarded the certificate. + or -

3.  If ........................, you will *not* get a traffic ticket. + or -

4.  If ........................, you will *not* have to attend Saturday school to make up the time. + or -

5.  If ........................, you will *not* be fined. + or -

6.  If .................... ..., you will *not* be allowed to attend the pep rally. + or -

7.  If ........................, your par score will *not* increase. + or -
    (Remember, in the game of golf, you want a low score.)

8.  If ........................, you will *not* have to depend on your friend for a ride. + or -

9.  If ........................, you will *not* be allowed to enter. + or -

10. If ........................, you will *not* be denied entrance. + or -

11. If ........................, you will *not* be counted tardy. + or -

12. If ........................, you will *not* be counted absent. + or -

Did you find that some words, which are already negative by meaning, convey a positive effect when combined with a *not*?

# NAND Logic Both Ways

As you have learned, NAND logic is logic in which two or more conditions must be met before there is "no" outcome. More specifically, you have NAND logic when the outcome is opposite the two inputs. Remember earlier in this book, when it was pointed out that conditions can be stated either positively or negatively and outcomes can be stated either positively or negatively? The previous two examples stated the conditions in the positive and the outcomes were that something would *not* happen. Let's look now at a NAND situation in which the statements are shown both ways: as before, when the conditions were positive; and now (in example #2), when the conditions are stated negatively and the outcome is positive.

| #1. **Condition (stated positively)** | **Outcome (stated negatively)** |
|---|---|
| IF it *is* raining | |
| AND | THEN We will *NOT* go to the picnic |
| IF it *is* too cold | |

| #2. **Condition (stated negatively)** | **Outcome (stated positively)** |
|---|---|
| IF it is *not* raining | |
| AND | THEN We *will* go to the picnic |
| IF it is *not* too cold | |

One could agree or disagree that the conditions in example #2 are negative conditions. Some may feel that "raining" has a negative meaning; therefore, "not raining" is a positive thing. However, if you were a farmer and your crops needed rain, "raining" would not be a negative concept. The same goes for "too cold." This is clearly a value judgment. Some people like to picnic in the snow!

Here's another example. Note the situation statement for this one.

Laurie wants to go to the mall. Her father tells her that if she is not still ill and if she doesn't have a game on Saturday, he will take her to the mall.

| **Condition (stated negatively)** | **Outcome (stated positively)** |
|---|---|
| IF Laurie is *not* ill | |
| AND | THEN Her father *will* take her to the mall |
| IF Laurie *doesn't* have a game | |

# (Advanced)
# Making NAND Logic

**Activity #15**

In the following NAND situations, fill in the conditions or outcomes, remembering to make them the inverse of each other.

1.  IF there is no school

    AND                    THEN You *will* go sledding

    _____


2.  IF _____

    AND                    THEN You *will not* get behind in your studies

    _____


3.  IF it is not raining

    AND                    THEN You *will* go _____

    IF it is not cloudy

4.  IF _____ not _____

    AND

    IF _____ not _____

                           THEN You *will* order in pizza

5.  IF _____

    AND                    THEN You *will not* need a ride

    _____

## Searching Databases with NAND Strategies

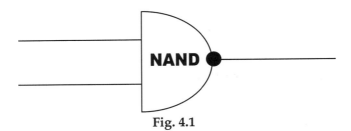

**Fig. 4.1**

You have learned that searching with AND logic is *exclusive* rather than inclusive. Because the word is "and," which means one thing *with* another, one might guess that an AND search would include all things of each kind together. However, you learned that this is not the case. An AND search includes only database items that include *both* descriptors, not one or the other.

With NAND (fig. 4.1), any database search you do will become even more exclusive. That means it will leave out more information and will include less. Here's how it works. Remember the example about "cats AND dogs"? Now let's make a search for the same thing, but with a different idea in mind. Let's say that last time we identified several books for use by veterinarians who work with cats and dogs, but also with cattle, horses, and sheep. We spent time sorting out books that did not refer to house pets. So let's try again. This time, our database will let us search with an expanded "descriptor set." We can now use both AND and NOT.

We begin with thinking like this: "I want books about dogs and cats as pets, but not books that include larger animals." So you begin your search like this:

Descriptors: cats AND dogs, NOT cattle

By adding the phrase "NOT cattle," you are eliminating more items from your search than would otherwise have come up. By adding more descriptors and ruling out other possibilities, you are saving yourself time and work by pinpointing exactly which books, articles, and other items are most likely to give you what you are looking for. Ask your teacher or librarian to help you find a database that will allow you to search with "AND, NOT" strategies.

Here are some more to think about.

1. Athletes AND sports figures, NOT swimmers
2. Band AND orchestra, NOT marching
3. Woodwinds AND instruments, NOT percussion

Can you think of some more?

**Activity #16**

# NAND Logic
# at Lunchtime

NAND logic is as near as the school cafeteria, corner ice cream shop, or fast-food restaurant. Follow the first example and decide how you like your snack!

Example:

Ice cream sundae

hot fudge AND marshmallow creme, NOT nuts

Now you try!

1.  Taco

    _____ AND _____, NOT _____

2.  Sub sandwich

    _____ AND _____, NOT _____

3.  Hamburger

    _____ AND _____, NOT _____

4.  Hot dog

    _____ AND _____, NOT _____

5.  Baked potato bar

    _____ AND _____ AND _____, NOT _____

# Chapter 5

# Your Choice: OR

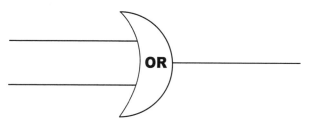

**Fig. 5.A. Logic symbol for "OR"**

So far you have learned about George Boole and his system of logic that lays the groundwork for modern computer logic. You have learned about If-Then statements, conditions and outcomes, and inputs and outputs. You have learned about stating conditions and outcomes negatively and positively. In addition, you have learned about the kind of logic George Boole called AND logic and the kind of logic that reverses the AND situation by adding a NOT logic, called NAND (NOT, AND). You also learned about NOT logic, which you found to be an inverse or opposite outcome to a condition. Next, you will learn a more inclusive logic.

*Situation #1:* You want to go to the high school basketball game. Your parents say OK, but you must find a friend to drive you because they cannot get free to take you. Here are your choices:

Conditions: Your older brother might be persuaded to take you and he can drive, but he will probably be taking his girlfriend. Your neighbor, who is your best friend, may be going with his family. If you want to go badly enough, you can begin to ask around. Here is how your situation looks diagrammed.

| **Condition** | **Outcome** |
|---|---|
| IF go with brother | |
| OR | THEN Go to the game |
| IF go with neighbor | |

In this situation, only one condition must be met. You have a choice! You could go with either your brother OR your neighbor. Either one will work—you don't need both.

*Situation #2:* Last year your best friend was on the Math Counts team and she loved it. This year you would like to try for that team. Here are the requirements to be considered for the team:

| **Conditions** | **Outcome** |
|---|---|
| IF train three months with the practice team | |
| OR | THEN Become a candidate for the practice team |
| IF have a 94 average or higher in math | |

You have a choice! If you do not have a 94 average, do you still have a chance to be a candidate for the math team? What else can you do? Can you see that either one condition *or* the other will work for you? This is an OR logic situation.

The truth table for Situation #2 would look like table 5.1. This table should be read from the top down.

| IF | | | | |
|---|---|---|---|---|
| Train three months? | yes | yes | no | no |
| OR | | | | |
| Have 94 average? | yes | no | yes | no |
| THEN | | | | |
| Qualify for math team? | yes | yes | yes | no |

**Table 5.1**

The truth table shows us that in three of the four situations, a condition is met that satisfies and brings forth the desired outcome. In the first IF column, both conditions are met, but that is more than is necessary to bring about the outcome. In the second and third columns, only one condition is met, but that is still enough to bring about the desired outcome, because of OR. In the fourth column, neither condition is met, so the outcome is not realized. When compared to the two-option AND logic examples you studied previously, you can see that OR logic allows more possibilities for success.

*Situation #3:* Your Scout troop has a fund-raiser under way. To earn the brightly colored patch for participation, you must help with the activity in one of several ways. It is your choice; just sign up for what you want to do!

**Conditions**                                          **Outcome**
IF
Sell popcorn door to door
        OR
Place prior notice of the sale in              THEN Earn participation patch
    the newspaper
        OR
Unload the trucks on delivery day
        OR
Help with the final accounting

You can see by this example how very different the OR situation is from the AND-logic situations that we analyzed previously. Clearly, any one of the listed conditions would satisfy the situation and bring about the desired outcome. There is no need for all of the conditions to be met, because of the OR logic. Your range of options and chances of meeting your goal are expanded (see table 5.2).

no = (-) yes = (+)

| IF | | | | | | | | | |
|---|---|---|---|---|---|---|---|---|---|
| Sell popcorn? | + | + | + | + | + | - | - | - | ... |
| **OR** | | | | | | | | | |
| Newspaper ad? | + | + | + | - | - | + | - | + | ... |
| **OR** | | | | | | | | | |
| Unload truck? | - | + | + | - | + | - | + | - | ... |
| **OR** | | | | | | | | | |
| Accounting? | + | - | + | + | - | - | - | + | ... |
| **THEN** | | | | | | | | | |
| Earn patch? | + | + | + | + | + | + | + | + | ... |

**Table 5.2**

The truth table for Situation #3 (table 5.2) is not complete. As you can see, there is no column showing "no" for every condition, although that certainly is a possibility. There are also other combinations of conditions that are not listed here. Can you identify at least one set of conditions not listed? How many more combinations of conditions could there be?

You can see that the *more* conditions there are, the more possibilities there are for the goal to be met. This is very different from AND logic, in which the more conditions there are, the *less* chance there is that the goal will be met.

**Activity #17**

# This Chore
# OR/AND That!

Let's put OR logic to work! Imagine that your family has a plan for keeping the house tidy. A parent has made the rule that after dinner you must do at least one chore for the family, and then you may come back to the table for a special dessert. But there is so much that you could do! List 10 chores that you could do around the house to earn that special dessert. (You could be an extra-special family member one evening and do even more!)

IF

1. _____, OR

2. _____, OR

3. _____, OR

4. _____, OR

5. _____, OR

6. _____, OR

7. _____, OR

8. _____, OR

9. _____, OR

10. _____, THEN Yum-yum

Now let's compare the OR logic to the AND logic that you learned previously. Let's imagine that your parents give you a quarter every day for doing three jobs around the house. That is an AND logic. To earn the quarter you must do these three things:

IF

1. _____, AND

2. _____, AND

3. _____, THEN 25 cents richer

# Boolean Logic: OR and the Parallel Circuit

Just as you learned about AND logic, it is important to see how OR logic can be used in computer circuitry and programming to make decisions. Remember that AND logic is used in *series* circuits, where all switches along the loop must be closed for the current to flow. Now, with OR logic, let's look at a different kind of circuit. This common circuit is called a *parallel* circuit. The circuit design in figure 5.1 shows two switches. Look carefully at the design of the circuit, though, and you will see that the two switches are independent of each other. This is a very different concept from what you saw with the AND circuit. Trace around the parallel circuit in the figure, starting at the batteries, and you will see that there are two ways to get to the lamp. You can choose either path. Either choice will connect the circuit and light the lamp. When either switch is closed, the lamp will light.

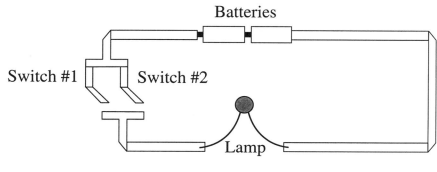

**Fig. 5.1**

The symbol in figure 5.2 represents two possible inputs and one output (result), just as the diagram in figure 5.1 shows.

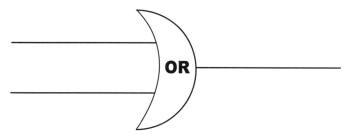

**Fig. 5.2**

Let's chart the logic of this circuit in a truth table (table 5.3).

| IF | | | | |
|---|---|---|---|---|
| Switch #1 | on | off | on | off |
| OR | | | | |
| Switch #2 | on | on | off | off |
| THEN | | | | |
| Lamp | on | on | on | off |

**Table 5.3**

Just as with the everyday logic situations we discussed before, with OR logic there are more opportunities or combinations that allow the outcome to take place. That is because only one *or* the other switch must be closed to allow the lamp to light.

Once again, imagine that a parallel circuit can have any number of inputs. That is, it may (and often does) have three, four, five, or more inputs. The more conditions that are input, the greater the chance that the output will be activated.

Think about an electric garage door opener as an example of a parallel circuit. Chances are you can either push a button on a box in the garage *or* activate the remote unit to close or open the door. Either choice will work; it is OR logic.

IF
Remote handset
    OR                        THEN Garage door activates (goes up or down)
Manual pushbutton

# Holding Back the Water in the Dam: Ready OR Not

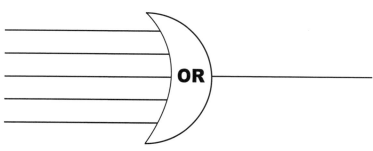

**Fig. 5.3. How many inputs does this OR circuit have?**

You have learned that computer circuits can receive input from other circuits and sensors. Let's put that concept to work by imagining that you are in control of the flood and release gates at a dam. Your control room receives information about various factors concerning the storage and release of water above the dam. Your main computer is constantly receiving data from sensors placed throughout the facility. Your main concerns are rainfall, wind, temperature, water flow, and water pressure against the wall of the dam. Altogether five circuits are reporting in. If any one of these sensors receives information that its measurement has exceeded (predetermined) safety levels, an alarm will sound and you must respond by altering the containment in some way. Using the preceding information, write the OR situation here:

1. IF _____ exceeds safety level,

    OR

2. IF _____ exceeds safety level,

    OR

3. IF _____ exceeds safety level,

    OR                                          THEN _____

4. IF _____ exceeds safety level,   —————————— .

    OR

5. IF _____ exceeds safety level,

# OR Logic As a Search Tool on a Computerized Database

OR logic is an underlying concept in database searching, just as AND logic is. OR logic can be used to search databases in school and public libraries and on the Internet as well.

As before, suppose that the librarian has all the books in the library entered in a database that is available to anyone by computer access. Your teacher has assigned you to write a paper on some aspect of the Civil War. You are on your own now (with a little help from your library's computer). As you study the search parameters on the school's computer, you see that you have choices about how to do the search. You have already learned how to search using AND and NAND. But because you may write on any topic, you need to find books that give you a variety of information, so that you can choose what interests you the most. To begin, you might enter the following descriptors or keywords into the search tool on the computer.

Find: generals OR slavery OR Lincoln OR battles

Do you think you will get a lot of hits? (That means, will the computer search turn up many books for you?) Chances are that quite a lot of books will be identified. Look closely and you can see that *any* book chosen need not include *all* of the topics you have identified. Rather, *any* book that has *any* of the keyword topics qualifies for identification. Now you will have your work cut out for you! Browse through the books and narrow down your topic to the one that interests you the most. Ask your teacher or librarian if you may try an OR search on the computer at your school or public library.

Syntax for searching with Boolean OR logic with any given search engine may vary, as it did with AND. Once again you must learn the appropriate syntax before using a major search engine, by entering the HELP or search tips menu. The traditional approach is to write the keywords and Boolean operator (in this case OR) as follows:

Fredericksburg OR Petersburg

Two variations of this syntax are common. Alta Vista, a very large search engine available through Internet access, will accept the word OR or a | mark between words. So the preceding example could also be entered as:

Fredericksburg | Petersburg

Note that this kind of OR search looks exactly like a pipe search (discussed in chapter 3). This emphasizes how important it is to check the syntax rules for a search before you use any particular search engine.

Infoseek and Lycos, two other large search engines, will assume "OR" if terms are entered with only a space between them:

Fredericksburg Petersburg Spotsylvania

This entry would identify information on *any one* of these Civil War battles. Each citation may have only one match, and will not necessarily contain either of the other two terms, because it is an OR search.

# AND Gets You Less, OR Gets You More! Comparing AND and OR Search Strategies

Even though it seems that the word AND should indicate that more things are included, you have learned that when you search with AND in a Boolean logic search, you actually exclude many references and include only those that have all of the search terms you specified. So remember, *AND gets you less!*

An OR search will find more books, articles, or sites that could possibly help you. When searching with Boolean OR logic, you are setting up the search to retrieve any book (or Web site) that includes the search term you have entered. *OR gets you more!*

Using the last example, in which you were asked to write a paper about the Civil War, we can see that perhaps both AND logic and OR logic may be helpful.

When you searched by the word "generals," you probably found many biographies about generals from all periods of time and in both wartime and peacetime. What you really needed was an AND logic search that would limit the number of responses the database returned:

> Find: generals AND Civil War

> Or, if you decided on famous battles, you could search:
> Find: battles AND Civil War

> Or, if you decided to focus on Lincoln:
> Find: Lincoln AND Civil War

> Or, if you decided to focus on slavery:
> Find: slavery AND Civil War

AND gets you less, but OR gets you more! (Remember, you may not always want more. Learn to know when you want fewer references and when you want more.)

**Activity #19**

# Designing OR Searches

Here are some search topics. Using what you have learned about Boolean logic searches with AND and OR, decide which topic will yield more hits (references in the library or on the Internet). Write *more* or *fewer* in the blanks.

1.  presidents AND premiers _____

    presidents OR premiers _____

2.  floods AND tornadoes _____

    floods OR tornadoes _____

3.  cars OR trucks _____

    cars AND trucks _____

4.  subways AND trains _____

    subways OR trains _____

5.  Broadway OR theater _____

    Broadway AND theater _____

6.  radio OR television _____

    radio AND television _____

7.  Now, think of some examples of your own:

    _____ OR _____

    _____ AND _____

From *Decision Points: Boolean Logic for Computer Users and Beginning Online Searchers.*
© 1999 Libraries Unlimited, Inc. (800) 237-6124

# Searching with Synonyms: Another Use for OR

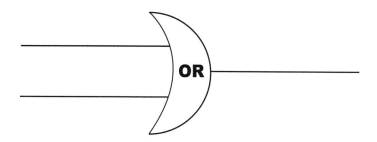

You have seen that "OR gets you more" and can be a useful operator to call in information on various topics, such as dogs OR cats. But let's suppose that you want to target only one topic. How can OR help you if you want to know about only cats?

The answer is to think in synonyms! Synonyms are words with the same or similar meanings. Maybe you can identify more books and articles if you include other words with similar meanings in your search.

For example, find two other words that could substitute for *cat*.

|  |  | **synonym** |  | **synonym** |
|---|---|---|---|---|
| cat | OR | feline | OR | kitten |

When doing a search for "cat," you could also include the search terms "feline" and "kitten," which may call up more items on your topic. You would write the search like this:

|  |  | **synonym** |  | **synonym** |
|---|---|---|---|---|
| cat | OR | feline | OR | kitten |

Now let's do a synonym search for "dog."

|  |  | **synonym** |  | **synonym** |
|---|---|---|---|---|
| dog | OR | canine | OR | puppy |

Remember, using synonyms with OR searching gives you the opportunity to find different books, articles, and other items that use different terminology but deal with the same topic.

**Activity #20**

# Synonym Searching
# with OR

Try these synonym searches with OR. Put each word in the list at the bottom of the page into the correct blank in the Synonym column.

Search term                    Synonym

1. ocean      OR  _____

2. horse      OR  _____

3. rain       OR  _____

4. gale       OR  _____

5. rocks      OR  _____

6. earth      OR  _____

7. aquanaut   OR  _____

8. astronomy  OR  _____

9. homes      OR  _____

10. rocket    OR  _____

Choose from:

a. stones        d. sea          g. equestrian      j. spaceship

b. hurricane     e. stars        h. precipitation

c. SCUBA         f. environment  i. habitats

# OR Logic Using Partial-Word Searching

Another search technique using Boolean OR does not actually use the term OR, but does use the concept. Partial-word searching, sometimes called *truncation*, is accomplished by identifying a keyword (most often a root word) and instructing to the computer to search *any* word with that root. In some databases and search engines, this is done by placing an asterisk (*) after the word. Think of it as providing the trunk of a tree and searching for its branches. For example, the entry electr* would yield (among others):

electricity   electric chair   electricians   electric eel   electric trains

electric motors   electrically   (and possibly) electronics (depending on which search engine you use)

Can you find the root *electr* in all of these words and phrases? This search can be interpreted as using a form of Boolean OR because it requests the search engine to find "electr" OR any other form of that word.

As you can see from the example, truncation can call up many different words that begin with *electr*. Those words may be associated with other words in phrases such as "electric eel"; others may be single word items. One database yielded 28 million hits for *electr.* *. Truncation would not be a strategy to use if you were searching for a specific word or phrase. It is most useful when you want to "cast a very large net" and gather anything that is available to be caught.

# (Advanced) Partial-Word Searching: Truncation

In a partial-word search using truncation, the search identifies the exact letters in the keyword. Circle any of the words that would be called up by a partial-word search for:

1. **season***

| fall season | unseasonable | pre-season | post-season |
| seasonal | winter | spring | Season's Greetings |

2. **poison***

| copperhead | nonpoisonous | rattlesnake | arsenic |
| poisonous | poisonous gases | poisonous snakes | carbon monoxide |

3. **elect***

| elected officials | senator | elections | elite fighters |
| Congress | electric circuits | electronics | electrocuted |
| elements | | | |

4. **marine***

Marine Corps    mariner    marina    submarine    marinade

5. Write five words that would be identified in a search for: **civil***
   (Use a dictionary if needed. Remember, this partial-word search could call up phrases as well.)

6. Write three words that would be identified in a search for: **rest***

# Chapter 6

# NOR Logic: Combining OR and NOT

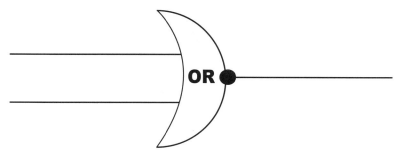

**Fig. 6.A. Logic symbol for "NOR"**

To this point you have seen the combination of two Boolean terms, NOT and AND, and how they can work together to express a more specific notion than either one standing alone. This is called NAND logic. Next we discussed NOR logic, a combination of NOT and OR, which is also used in everyday logic, computer circuitry, and database and Web searching.

## Using NOR Logic with Affirmative and Negative Statements

Remember when you learned about NOT logic? You learned that it is a reversal, a negation, or a negative consequence to an action. For example, "If you make a D in English, you will *not* play sports." NOR logic uses NOT in much the same way, but instead of one or more conditions preceding the "*not*" outcome, any condition of several possibilities can cause the *not* outcome.

IF the car door is open

    OR                THEN The car will *not* start

IF the seat belt is off


IF the road is icy

    OR                THEN We will *not* camp out at the national park

IF it snows


IF it rains

    OR                THEN We will *not* go to the zoo

IF it is too cold

You can add more conditions, too:

IF the road is icy
    OR
IF it snows
    OR           THEN We will *not* go camping in the national park
IF five people don't attend
    OR
IF there is a winter storm
    watch in effect

Check this scenario on a truth table (see table 6.1). Read the columns on this table from the top down. Not all possibilities are listed.

no = (-)   yes = (+)

| IF | | | | | | | | | |
|---|---|---|---|---|---|---|---|---|---|
| Road icy? | + | - | - | - | - | + | - | + | ... |
| OR | | | | | | | | | |
| Snows? | - | - | + | - | - | + | + | - | ... |
| OR | | | | | | | | | |
| Enough people? | - | - | - | + | - | + | + | - | ... |
| OR | | | | | | | | | |
| Storm watch? | - | - | - | - | + | + | - | + | ... |
| THEN | | | | | | | | | |
| Go camping? | - | + | - | - | - | - | - | - | ... |

**Table 6.1**

You can see from this truth table that your chances of getting to go camping get slimmer as more conditions become involved.

## Searching with OR and NOT

Suppose someone you know is shopping for a new car. Because she lives in hot, mountainous terrain, she wants her new car to have certain features. Front-wheel drive helps improve traction on various road conditions, so it is a desirable option, as is air-conditioning to keep out the dust and cool the interior of the vehicle.

Your friend looks at several vehicles and then tells the salesperson she wants:

Front-wheel drive
    OR           NOT Rear-wheel drive
Four-wheel drive
(which includes front-wheel drive)

This is NOR logic. By using these logic terms, she has moved closer to a decision point by ruling out rear-wheel-drive vehicles. The salesperson can then narrow down the possibilities of vehicles that will please this customer.

Your friend further tells the salesperson that she wants either:

A sedan
   OR                      NOT A pickup truck
A mini-van

By giving these descriptors to the salesperson, she reaches another decision point, and her choices have been narrowed once again. After various other discussions, the final decision is reached:

White
   OR
Tan                       NOT Black
   OR
Blue

The salesperson now knows specifically what is acceptable to this customer. If a database of area dealerships and their stock is available, the salesperson might enter something like this:

White mini-van
   OR                     NOT Rear-wheel drive
Blue mini-van

NOR logic helps to narrow choices and come closer to a decision point.

# How Would You Like That Served? Making NOR Decisions

Follow the example in #1 and write some details about everyday NOR decisions. See if these choices sound familiar OR delicious!

1.  How do you like your baked potato?

    Sour cream

        OR         NO(T) chives

    Butter

2.  How do you like your hamburger served?

    Catsup

        OR         NO(T) _____

    Mustard

3.  How do you like your tacos?

    _____

        OR         NO(T) _____

    _____

4.  How do you like your sub sandwiches?

    _____

        OR         NO(T) _____

    _____

5.  How do you like your ice cream sundaes?

    _____

        OR         NO(T) _____

    _____

# In the Deli with NAND

In Activity #22 you helped yourself to a large serving of NOR decisions. Find out how easily these same situations can be turned into NAND-logic situations. Study the example here and then follow through in questions 1 to 4 to change the previous NOR logic to NAND logic.

Example:

How do you like your baked potato? (NAND)

sour cream AND butter, NOT chives

sour cream AND butter AND bacon bits, NOT chives

(How many more things do you like on your potato?)

1.  How do you like your hamburgers? (NAND)

    a. _____ AND _____, NOT _____

    b. _____ AND _____ AND _____, NOT _____

2   How do you like your tacos? (NAND)

    a. _____ AND _____, NOT _____

    b. _____ AND _____ AND _____, NOT _____

3.  How do you like your sub sandwiches? (NAND)

    a. _____ AND _____, NOT _____

    b. _____ AND _____ AND _____, NOT _____

Remember, the language you use defines the logic needed, and the decision point is the result!

Activity #24

# Database Searching with NOR

## AND gets you less and OR gets you more! AND needs all, but OR takes any.

What about when you add a NOT to an OR? Using a search topic that was previously shown for an OR search (cars OR trucks), remember you will get hits that include *all* items about cars and *all* items about trucks. But watch what happens when you add a NOT qualifier to OR.

cars OR trucks NOT semitrailer trucks

You will still get the same books and articles about cars, but now you have eliminated some of the truck items because you requested no semi-trucks. Most searching systems will identify all of the hits for "cars" and all of the hits for "trucks" first; then they will go through those and strip away the ones that refer to semitrailer trucks. In that way, fewer articles will be identified. A word of caution: You may also have directed the computer to delete some very good items about trucks, just because you did not want hits with semitrailer trucks. Always be sure to think through what it is you really want to identify before you define your search terms and operators (AND, OR, NAND, NOR).

Use NOR when OR gets you too much and you want to exclude data from your search. Try these:

1.   presidents OR premiers NOT Congress

2.   Olympics OR World Games NOT national competitions

3.   golf OR tennis NOT _____

4.   pets OR dogs NOT _____

5.   ducks OR chickens NOT _____

Can you think of more?

From *Decision Points: Boolean Logic for Computer Users and Beginning Online Searchers.*
© 1999 Libraries Unlimited, Inc. (800) 237-6124

# Alternative Notations for NOR—Advanced

As explained earlier in this book, syntax rules for searching vary from search engine to search engine. Activity #24 used the most widely accepted syntax: a straightforward, left-to-right sequence with all the words written out:

girls OR children NOT adults
entrees OR meals NOT seafood
appetizers OR antipasto NOT desserts

In some search systems, the (-) sign can be used in place of NOT. Another way to write these would be to use the - sign as follows:

girls OR children -adults
entrees OR meals -seafood
appetizers OR antipasto -desserts
cobblers OR pies -strawberry

Some search engines provide a template such as

|  | OR |  | - |  |
|---|---|---|---|---|
|  | OR |  | NOT |  |

There are variations among search engines on how to enter the search terms. Check the search engine you are using to find out its preference.

Because some major search engines assume OR, you could use:

girls children -adults
entrees meals -seafood
appetizers antipasto -desserts

As you saw before, Alta Vista allows you to use the | sign. You can also use a *string* (a phrase) to remove unwanted material:

snakes OR pythons NOT "Monty Python"

This search would rule out any reference to *Monty Python's Flying Circus*, the television show, thus focusing on the reptilian meaning.

Not all search systems are *case-sensitive*—that is, they may or may not count differences in upper- and lower-case letters as significant. In some search systems, though, another way to differentiate between word meanings is by using capital letters:

dolphins OR porpoises NOT Dolphins

This search is intended to rule out all references to the Miami Dolphins, by using the capital letter connoting a proper noun. Here's another:

bison OR buffalo NOT Buffalo

This search is intended to focus on the mammals, not the city of Buffalo or the Buffalo Bills football team.

falcons OR hawks NOT Hawks

This search is intended to focus on birds of prey rather than the Atlanta Hawks basketball team.

marine OR sea NOT Marine

This search is intended to focus on sealife and aquatic issues, and to exclude articles about the Marine Corps.

# (Advanced)
# Excluding Information with NOT

Fill in the blanks in the following exercises. Be careful of double meanings, so that you exclude unwanted meanings from the search.

1. _____ OR _____ NOT "Maple Leafs" (referring to the Toronto ice hockey team)

2. _____ OR _____ NOT Seahawks

3. _____ OR _____ NOT Cardinals

4. _____ OR _____ NOT Bulls

5. _____ OR _____ NOT Hornets

(Remember, you can search for the same word as the one that is excluded by not using the capital letter. In that way you will get the basic noun, not the proper noun.)

For the following, describe what each search would yield and what is intended to be excluded.

6. crows OR blackbirds NOT "Counting Crows"

7. "Counting Crows" OR "pop-rock" NOT crows

8. race OR "civil rights" NOT cars

9. space OR architecture NOT outer

10. base OR acid NOT ball NOT baseball

# Chapter 7

# Combining AND and OR Logic to Make One Big Decision

Inside computers, the central processing units use small "chips," called *integrated circuits*, that are made up of simple circuits, both parallel and series. When a simple circuit is "integrated" (combined) with many others, the circuitry soon doesn't look simple anymore. If you use a microscope to look at the surface of a computer chip, you will see a universe of connections displayed. This complex intertwining of simpler circuit components gives us integrated circuits. Computer designers use the logic you have learned throughout this book to create computers that "make decisions" at the circuit level.

Let's explore, in everyday language, how the various logic concepts AND, OR, NAND, NOR, and If-Then are used during our day, every day! We'll use the language of Boolean algebra, descriptive situation statements, and electronic symbols for each example. We begin by looking at an *integrated* logic situation for AND/OR/AND and learning how to make a great fruit salad as well!

## Grandmother's Fruit Salad Bowl

*Statement:* To make this delicious salad, you will need a cup of canned peaches, a cup of sliced bananas, a cup of chunk pineapple, and either sour cream or yogurt for the dressing.

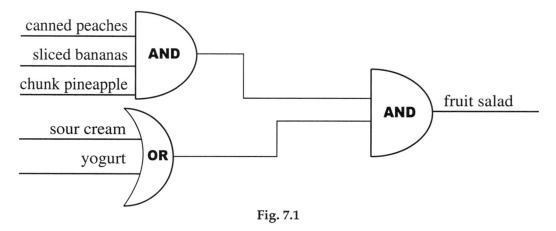

Fig. 7.1

Looking at this recipe, as diagrammed in figure 7.1, you see that three fruit ingredients are required (AND) and that there is a choice (OR) of salad dressing. These are then put together (AND) to complete the salad. The element of choice comes into play regarding the dressing for the salad. Can you see that this is really a recipe for two different kinds of salads?

In this same way, computer circuitry can take information into an AND circuit from an inputting circuit, no matter what kind of logic the input circuit is representing. Now watch as two AND logic situations "feed" into an OR logic situation, as a host and hostess plan hors d'oeuvres for a party (fig. 7.2).

## AND/AND/OR

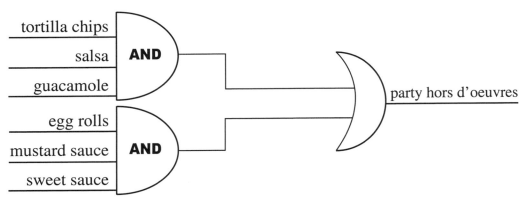

**Fig. 7.2**

This example shows that the hosts may decide to have one set of hors d'oeuvres or the other, or both. From this example, we would not know what to expect at the party, because the decision is left open. The OR logic brings choice to the party.

Let's try a situation with OR/OR/OR/AND (fig. 7.3). Again, hope to be hungry!

*Statement:* At my Super Bowl party my guests can decide for themselves how to make their tacos.

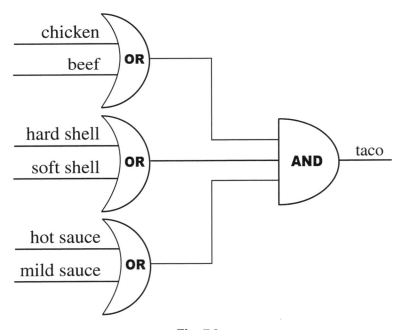

**Fig. 7.3**

## More Examples of Combined AND and OR Logic

*Statement:* To earn a child care merit badge for Scouting, you must fulfill the following requirements:

> Volunteer six hours in a child care facility
> OR
> Take a six-hour course on child care being offered at the hospital
> AND Show knowledge of how to change a diaper
> AND Tell about how to handle a baby safely
> AND Discuss the risks of choking on certain foods

This statement would be diagrammed as in figure 7.4.

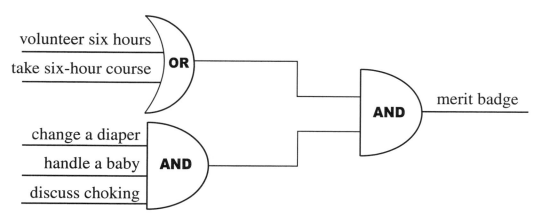

**Fig. 7.4**

*Statement:* To be on the Math Counts team, you must train for six months or score 90 or above on the pretests and be in the seventh or eighth grade.

This statement would be diagrammed as follows (fig. 7.5).

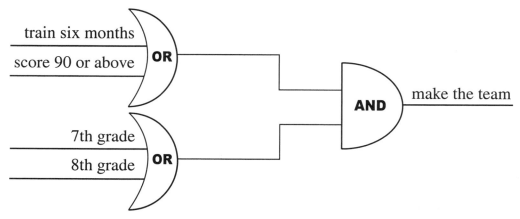

**Fig. 7.5**

*A public service announcement states:* Admission will be $1 to the Slammers game Friday night for each person who comes with a food donation to the Golden Harvest Food Bank. Bring either three cans of vegetables, five pounds of flour, or a canned meat product and admission will be only $1. If you bring any of the above items and the coupon from this week's *Herald Star*, then admission will be free.

This statement can be diagrammed as in figure 7.6.

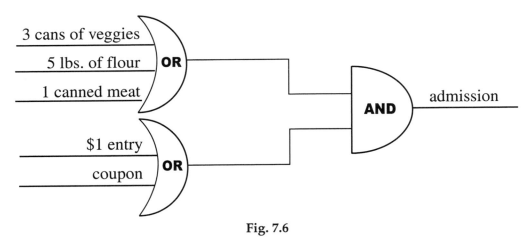

**Fig. 7.6**

Look for the Boolean expressions embedded in the language of this statement. You will find OR, AND, and If-Then. These words define the conditions of admission.

*Your teacher writes this on the board:* Complete problems 1–40 (even numbers) or 1–40 (odd numbers) and one brain teaser, either #4 or #5.

This statement can be diagrammed as in figure 7.7.

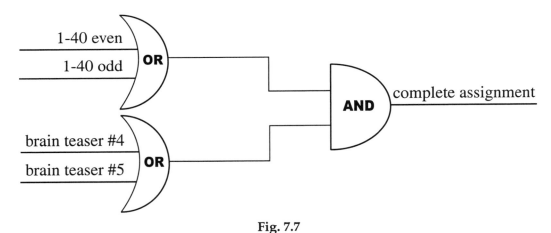

**Fig. 7.7**

Again, try to find the Boolean terms OR and AND in this assignment statement.

*Statement:* To be eligible for entrance to the Higher Learning Academy, you must have completed two years of a foreign language, either French or German; two years of a science, either biology or chemistry; four years of English; and one year each of geometry and algebra (See fig. 7.8).

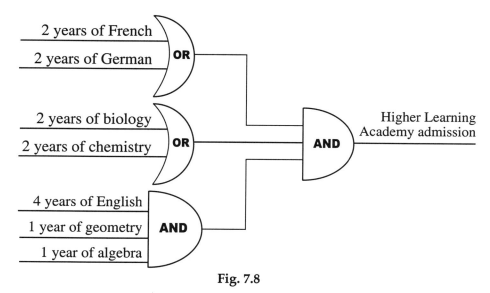

**Fig. 7.8**

*Statement:* You will be backpacking for three days in the mountains. You have to decide what gear is appropriate and can be carried for that length of time (See fig. 7.9).

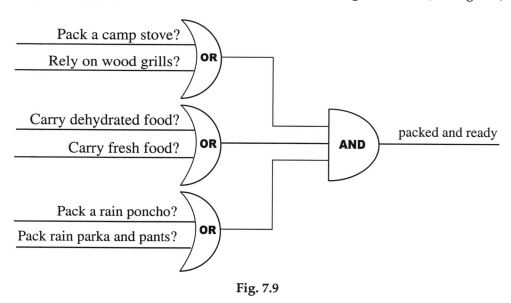

**Fig. 7.9**

Can you think of more?

**Activity #26**

# Using Logic Operators to Design Your Own Pizza

Suppose that, after your team wins a tournament, your coach treats the team to pizza at a nearby restaurant. As you order, you find that you must "decide" your way through various Boolean logic situations just to get the waiter to understand how the pizza (outcome) should be made.

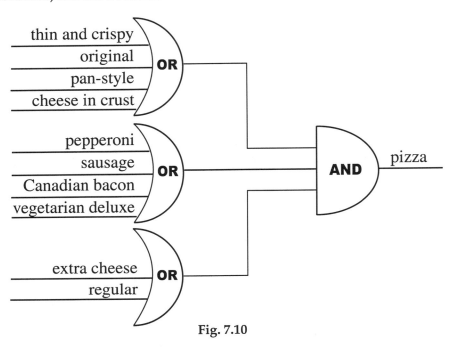

**Fig. 7.10**

Circle the choices you would make from the diagram in figure 7.10. On the following blanks, write in the descriptive terms from the diagram to show how you would order your pizza. Can you see that this is a three-input AND decision?

_____ AND _____ AND _____

Challenge: Did you notice that the OR logic for the pizza crust decision was not just the same as previous OR decisions? So far you have seen that *any* input or *all* of the inputs to an OR decision were acceptable. Here you find it is impossible to have thin and crispy and original and pan-style crust on the same pizza. Nor can you have "regular" and "extra cheese" at the same time, because they mean two different things. Electronic engineers have a special circuit, called an *Exclusive OR circuit*, that can accommodate this kind of situation. It allows only one of the OR choices to come through at a time.

*Activity #27*

# The Family Reunion

From the map in figure 7.11, make up a logic diagram that describes the choices made in deciding how to get to the family reunion.

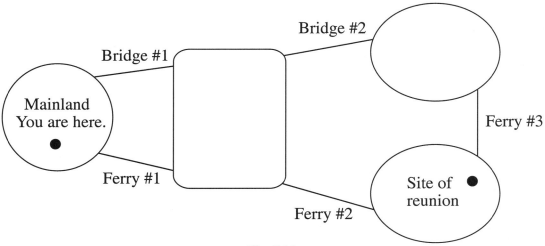

**Fig. 7.11**

There are four possible combinations:

| | | | | |
|---|---|---|---|---|
| Bridge #1 | AND | Bridge #2 | AND | Ferry #3 |
| | OR | | | |
| Ferry #1 | AND | Ferry #2 | | |
| | OR | | | |
| Ferry #1 | AND | Bridge #2 | AND | Ferry #3 |
| | OR | | | |
| Bridge #1 | AND | Ferry #2 | | |

Reach destination!

Now that you have identified four possible ways to reach the destination, a decision still has to be made. What factors would help you choose one way over another? Are you trying to save money? Do you get seasick on boats? Do you want to go the fastest way? Do you want to see dolphins on the way? Can you think of any other factors that would influence your choice? With an OR logic operator, the decision is up to you!

# The Final Decision

Now you are familiar with Boolean logic and its use as search operators. You have learned how computers make decisions one step at a time. You have also seen the similarity between the computer decision-making process and everyday decision situations.

At this point you may wonder: Is it necessary to define each step in a decision process in our daily lives? Probably not. Some decisions are commonplace and have been made many times, so that the "correct" decision has been learned (e.g., taking your umbrella if it is raining; taking your sunscreen if it is sunny). Human beings have a natural ability to learn and remember familiar patterns of conditions and outcomes and to make decisions based on previous experiences. Luckily, the human brain does not need to analyze every choice presented throughout a day, but can rely on this previous learning. Computers usually don't have the ability to learn from previous patterns, and so must analyze each new decision by its input. For each analysis, Boolean logic allows computers to reason effectively.

Even for humans, though, there are many situations in which the decision process is more complex. Using the models of logic in this book, you can now analyze conditions and possible outcomes for many decisions that you face. This analysis will help you make better, more informed choices. The final decisions are still up to you.

# Chapter 8

## Knowledge in the Information Age

Finding and managing information to increase knowledge is the challenge of the current age. This trend will continue. Increasingly, new jobs require computer-based knowledge skills; nearly 60 percent of new jobs require knowledge workers. It is estimated that approximately every two years, the quantity of information in the world doubles. In addition, the time it takes for that information to double is steadily shrinking. Such rapid change inevitably means that some part of what we believe to be true is no longer correct. Further, some part of what we need to know has already been made public, but we have not yet found it. These next chapters explore new systems for knowing, systems that help to meet these information needs. In particular, it shows how to take the Boolean thinking skills you have learned so far and use them with the world's information systems. This includes information systems both on personal computers and across the world's growing networks of computers. By effectively using these new systems, learners of all ages can thrive, not merely survive, amidst the coming challenges of the new century.

Finding information is the first stage of the information management process. It is possible that the number of power search tools is growing at an even faster rate than the amount of information. These electronic power tools do help to keep paths cut through the burgeoning forest of data. By following these paths we can find what we need. However, the use of power tools has its own problems. It is challenging to stay current on their options and features. Further, search tools frequently deliver far more information than is needed, and the information received is too often not exactly what the searcher intended. It is as if you ordered a toothpick of white pine but found an entire truckload of yellow pine logs dumped at your doorstep. Boolean logic acts as an administrator that keeps the powerful search tools under more effective control.

Once you find information, you must move on to new stages of the process. Knowing facts without organizing and acting on them means that the effort of hunting for them was often wasted. The process by which we turn facts into something useful requires other thinking skills: recalling, reorganizing (critical thinking), and generating knowledge (creative thinking). For a more detailed exploration of this thinking complex, examine the very thorough Integrated Thinking Model published by the Iowa Department of Education (1989), the LEAP model (Houghton 1995), and other works that integrate learning, teaching, thinking skills, and new technologies (Houghton 1998; Jonassen 1996). The more effectively you manage the first stage of finding information, the more powerful the end result will be when you share your solution. Cycling through different stages helps grow new knowledge, and Boolean logic assists decisions at each stage.

The process of looking for or finding information can also be thought of as the process of hunting. From this perspective, this information-age problem has brought us full circle, from the edge of the twenty-first century back to the dawn of human history. Then as now, key decisions must be addressed in establishing how best to proceed when preparing to hunt and during hunting. In this book, these decision points in information gathering are addressed and explored as a series of question statements and are answered in the context of our century:

Why hunt?
Who does the hunting?
Where do I hunt?
When do I hunt?
What do I hunt?
How do I hunt?
How do I store and use what I have caught? (see chapter 11)

## Why Hunt?

We hunt for information when we are hungry for knowledge. We hunt for the fun of the exploration. We hunt to improve our hunting skills. We hunt to test new hunting tools. With new tools we will gather more with the same effort, or for less effort we can be as effective as before. The rate of growth in our forest of information is so high that we need to hunt often just to keep current with the good paths, pitfalls, and shifting opportunities.

We also hunt to teach others. We teach others to hunt not just because it is good for them, but because it is good for the "tribe," which is our community and our culture. Others who hunt bring us new ideas. Eventually those who do not learn to hunt will have to rely on the hunting and storage systems of others. Hunting for information-age "wild game" can be as social and inviting an event as earlier forms of the hunt.

## Who Does the Hunting?

Those facing the problem of knowledge hunger must decide whether to head out into the forest of information themselves, hire a guide, employ a variety of more automated systems, or use others who are more experienced to do the hunting. In each of these cases, the effort can be free or for a fee. *Decision Points* assumes that you already have the basic equipment for the hunt. This means that you must own or have access to a personal computer that can connect to the Internet through a modem or some direct connection. If you do not have a computer at home or in the classroom, find out where you can use one; many city and school libraries cover the basic costs of Internet access and make computers available to community members free of charge. This chapter shows you how to use this basic equipment to become more expert with the many hunting tools that are freely available.

## Where Do I Hunt?

Too often the attempt to gain information leads to searching an enormous database of computer files (e.g., search engine) on the global Internet first. Actually, a search strategy might best begin closer to home and work outward through the networks. For example, you can start with the hard drive of the computer you currently use. If you have been using this computer for a couple of years, you probably have tens of thousands of files on the hard drive and on computer diskettes. You may have already stored the data you need and forgotten that it exists.

All recent personal computer operating systems, including the commonly used Macintosh, Unix, and Windows operating systems, have a "find" command as a standard feature. This command allows you to search through the names of your computer files. Depending on the version of your computer system, different degrees of Boolean logic are available. At the most basic level, you can use the concept of truncation or partial-word searching to do a type of OR search. If you enter the term *cat*, the system will retrieve file names with *cat* in them, including *catch, firecat, catechism, cat*, and *catalog*. These operating systems also provide a variation of AND searching. They use a number of different file format features, including date of file, size of file, application that created it, and so forth. For example, you could search for all the files containing *cat* AND those written within the last three months. Such searches will also include a hunt through the data on any inserted diskettes, compact discs (CDs), and other local storage devices.

More complex searching goes beyond file names to look into the actual content of the files. Simple versions of file-content searching are available in Windows 95, Windows 98, and Macintosh OS 8.5. Special-feature software that is readily obtainable uses a wide range of Boolean and other features to find strings of text in word processing, database, and spreadsheet files. Retrieve It! from MVP Solutions is an example of such a program for the Macintosh computer. Wilbur, shareware from RedTree Development Inc., is such a program for the Windows series of operating systems. These same programs will also search attached storage devices such as inserted diskettes and CDs.

Once the resources of the desktop computer are exhausted, hunters can expand their strategy to search their local area network of computers. Colleagues at work may have made portions of their computers' hard drives public, or have placed documents on file servers accessible to those in their institution. (Such a system is also referred to as an *intranet*.) The same programs that search the contents of the desktop computer's hard drive can also be told to search the drives of any networked computers. This is possible, though, only if their owners have set permission to allow remote access. For example, several colleagues may trade computer files by storing this information in special "public" folders to which each has the passwords.

There are many varieties of more extensive computer networks. These include systems on campuses, in communities, and regional and state systems. Each scale of network provides ways to search the public areas of its connected computers. The network that dwarfs all other networks is not truly a network, but a network of tens of thousands of networks. This awe-inspiring champion of cross-networked files and protocols is called the *Internet*. Its growth continues at a phenomenal rate, which some estimate as high as 10 to 20 percent a month. It has already become the premier electronic storage system for the planet. Much of this chapter is devoted to the capacity of the Internet.

## When Do I Hunt?

With your own computer, you have control over when you work. The issue of when to hunt arises when you require access to computers beyond your own. Your best hunting begins with access to the fastest telecommunication systems you can find. For most computer users, this means using a modem attached to a telephone line at home or in the office. Many institutions install special network wiring that allows computers to trade data much faster than modems on existing telephone lines. However, high numbers of users can slow the fastest system to a pace even slower than a home telephone modem.

Every year computer makers continue to increase the speed at which computers can internally process information. This internal speed is far faster than the speed at which computers can trade information with each other. The future of higher speed telecommunications generally depends on the quality of the connections that carry the information between computers. Larger institutions can more easily find the funding to install their own special wiring and long distance data services. Homes and smaller businesses must depend on community-wide systems, which are now racing to provide high-speed services. Telephone, cable television, and wireless service companies all have the technical capacity to do this. Telephone companies have a significant lead over their competitors in that they can at least provide slow-speed service right now. The changeover to high-speed lines has already be-gun in large metropolitan regions and will slowly spread outward into less populated areas. As high-speed systems reach even homes and small businesses in the future, the nature of the hunt will continue to change.

With the current capacity of networked computers, hunters can be about the business of global access anytime, 24 hours a day, 7 days a week. However, high numbers of users on a network can measurably slow the response time of your hunt. Some claim that when the West Coast begins business hours at 8 AM, Pacific Coast Time, the East Coast networks, at 11 AM Eastern Standard Time, slow down because of the increased traffic. This implies that early morning hours are best on the East Coast. Late afternoon hours are then best on the West Coast, as many of those in the East will have turned off their computers at work and gone home. However, the local area network in your office complex, building, or institution will generally have a far greater effect on your speed than national and international traffic. Within your local system, much depends on the number of users and how heavily they use the local network. Pay attention to your network speed, sometimes shown in the bottom of your browser window (as with Netscape or Internet Explorer). This number is expressed as some quantity of data over some period of time, such as 300 bytes per second or 2.5KB (2,500 bytes) per second. The higher the number, the faster the speed. To check whether your com-munication speed is the best possible, talk with neighbors and colleagues from time to time about their speeds. Further, whenever possible, avoid the times during the day or the days during the week on which speed is noticeably slower.

## What Do I Hunt?

What you hunt can be thought of as *data structures*. Data and information come in a wide range of shapes and sizes. Hunters need to be able to identify their game. Information can be stored and read as many different kinds of media, including text (e.g., magazine articles and printed books), photographs and other still images, movies, and audio. All of these media can be found as computer data or computer files. They may be mixed together and displayed on the same computer screen. That is, a computer may be able to simultaneously display text and a photograph while playing both sound and video. The computer can also use any of these media by themselves or in many other combinations.

Thinking about what you seek as data structures is not nearly as useful as thinking in terms of other generalizations. These different forms of data can also be thought of as People, Places, and Things. These objects of the hunt also suggest a priority in how you go about the act of hunting.

## How Do I Hunt?

The speed of computer networks is a factor over which you may have little control. Hunting strategy, often referred to in the Information Age as *search strategy*, is a factor over which computer users do have complete control. Good strategy is critical to success.

Early in the process of solving problems, the user looks for new information to better understand the problem. The main goal should be to present a concern or issue concisely as a question or declarative statement. Write down your search statement as a sentence. As you search, rewrite your search sentence in ways that make it clearer. The goal is to transform your thinking from a vague, fuzzy idea into a crisp outline of the target. When your search sentence is brief and clear, searching will become much more efficient. The more clearly you can define the target of the hunt, the easier it is to look for it.

Another key step in this phase of your problem solving is to select the information systems that will give you a chance to find the best data first, then move to lesser categories as the primary ones are exhausted. This provides a sequence for dealing with three broad categories of information systems, referred to here as Person, Place, or Thing.

It is useful at this point to see the levels of Person, Place, and Thing as if they were stacked in a pyramid. The top of the pyramid, the Person part, has the most capable judgment but generally the smallest quantity of information. The middle level, the Place part, contains books, articles, and other items that have been screened and qualified by editors and reviewers but require additional efforts to obtain. The bottom level, the Thing part, contains all the electronic documents of the Internet. Publication on the Internet may or may not involve review and critique by others. When searching for electronic documents on the Internet, heed the Latin phrase *caveat emptor*, which can now be translated as "searcher beware." Files can go directly from an individual's computer to Internet publication on an Internet-accessible computer's hard drive. The quantity of information that you can get your hands or eyes on immediately is far larger at the bottom of the pyramid than at the middle or top, but the quality of the Thing level ranges from rotten to excellent. Much greater responsibility is placed on the hunter to capture information of the highest quality.

The best strategy is to start at the top of this pyramid and work down through its levels of Person, Place, and Thing. To be effective, hunters must learn more about the tools for hunting at each of these levels. There is a problem, though, with writing about such a rapidly changing area. It is said that seven Internet years equal one human year. By the time the reader finds and works through this publication, some of the details of how these systems work will have changed. The Boolean logic discussed earlier will not have changed. Instead, the way different tools implement Boolean logic may vary. Consequently, the goal of this review of systems is not to be totally comprehensive about every detail of such tools. Rather, it will provide representative samples of how a variety of Internet-based tools use Boolean thinking to give users more effective control.

# References

Houghton, Robert S. 1995. *CROP: Meta-Doorway to the Information Age*. Online. [Available: http://www.resolving.com].

Houghton, Robert S. 1998. "Technological Leadership in Rural Schools." In *Leadership in Rural Education*. Lancaster, PA: Technomic Publishing.

Iowa Department of Education. 1989. *A Guide to Developing Higher Order Thinking Across the Curriculum*. Des Moines, IA: Department of Education. (ERIC Document Reproduction Service No. ED 306 550).

Jonassen, D. 1996. *Computers in the Classroom: Mindtools for Critical Thinking*. Englewood Cliffs, NJ: Prentice Hall.

# Chapter 9

# Person, Place, or Thing

The information system of greatest potential judgment and intelligence is another human being. The value of this judgment to the hunter depends on that human being's interest and expertise in the area of the problem, question, or topic. Human minds have a very important advantage over information printed on paper or found online: They can interact. Through such interaction they carry out several important steps, which include refocusing a question, selecting qualified information that is most relevant to your needs, and identifying what you do not need to find. Each of these actions can significantly reduce the time you spend searching. This customized interactivity is not inherent to the other two major levels of information that are discussed later.

There are several ways to unearth people's names and find their contact information. In the study of a topic, whether on Web pages or in a book, names will appear. These names can be as valuable as the content of the pages that those with more expertise provide. A search for relevant public institutions, businesses, and corporations will also lead to the people that are their employees. A search for electronic conferences in the area of your topic will also lead to the participants.

There are downsides to this approach. You do not know how long it will take to get a response, if you receive one at all. Businesses in the electronic advertising directories—the electronic Yellow Pages—of course are much more likely to respond quickly, but they may do so at a price. Truth is not guaranteed at this or any level of information pyramid. The three types of systems for electronic contact presented here are: the White Pages, Yellow Pages, and electronic conferences.

## White-Page Postal Address and Telephone Numbers

The White Pages link on Lycos's home page leads to their People Find Service (http://www.lycos.com/peoplefind/). It provides more than a dozen different databases in which you can search personal, business, and government names for telephone numbers and postal and email addresses. A reverse look-up feature also allows you to find names if you know other data; for example, enter a phone number to find its associated personal name or institution.

"Phone Number" is the title of one of the People Finder options. It uses a form of AND searching. The more fields you provide, the fewer matches it will retrieve. There are five types of data to enter: First Name, Last Name, City, State, and Country. Enter as many of these fields as possible and it will return as many names as match your conditions. For example, a search for Bill Clinton in the United States, without any data in City or State, returned 20 variations with the first name of Bill and William and their mailing addresses. If you do the search again after adding more data, the system will return fewer names. By adding the state of Texas to the data entered previously, a search found only two matches for Bill Clinton.

The "Phone Number" database is not a perfect match with local telephone directories or the telephone company information services. It is also possible that persons who have listed telephone numbers may choose to remove their names from the Internet searching system. When a number or address is not returned from the Internet, users should try the technologies that they previously used. The telephone company's information service is always available.

## White-Page Email Addresses

Yahoo! People Search (http://people.yahoo.com/) provides a Web form page for finding email addresses. The form also uses AND logic. For example, entering the first name of William and the domain name of .gov returned more than 200 names and their email addresses. As more of the form's boxes (categories) become filled, the further the search is narrowed. Repeating the search and adding the last name of Clinton to the search reduced the number of hits to 25. One of these returns was the address for a William Clinton of the White House, president@whitehouse.gov.

One interesting and useful feature of these directory (white-page) systems is a new standard for electronic address books. Each record of contact information, referred to as a vCard or virtual Rolodex card, can automatically be transferred from Internet contact databases to your own personal address books. (These address books are databases of contact information on your personal computer.) They are a part of Internet Web browsers such as Netscape, Internet Explorer, Outlook Express, and Sidekick 98. Some programs let you drag and drop from the Internet contact databases. Others may automatically detect the presence of a vCard and prompt you to add it to your address book.

## Yellow-Page Example

Advertising directory (Yellow Page) service is offered by many online companies. GTE maintains a site called BigBook (http://www.bigbook.com/). The default "simple search" asks for some combination of category, business name, city, and state or nation. But because the categories used often are not known by the searcher, it is better to scroll the page and find the link to the extra features of the Detailed Search page.

On the Detailed Search page is a button called Top Categories. Top Categories lists the most common categories, drawn from the Standard Industrial Classifications (SICs) developed by the U.S. government. If you want to choose several categories that might meet your needs, scroll through this long list and write down the most appropriate categories. If you click on a category, BigBook will automatically fill in the category field on the form. You can also type any useful word into the category field; if it is not one of the official categories, the program will attempt to give you a list of categories that are most relevant to what you are seeking.

Another special field on the Detailed Search page is the keyword field. This is another form of an OR search. Adding terms here will not narrow the search in the sense that items will be eliminated, but it can help you scan your results. Businesses that have listed specific products or services in their online Fact Files that match your keywords will be highlighted with a gold key in the returned search results. When using multiple keywords, separate them with commas. A number in the gold key indicates the number of matched keywords.

## Email Conferences

Both newsgroups and mailing lists (*listservs*) are forms of email conferences. *Email conferences*, which use different ways for groups of people to share email, are a means whereby those interested in similar subjects can "meet" and trade ideas, questions, and solutions. There are tens of thousands of such email conferences in English alone, and new ones form every day. If you send one email message to an email conference, everyone who participates in the conference can see it. This may mean that only a dozen participants see it, or it may mean that it will be seen by tens of thousands.

The two major types of email conferences differ in how the electronic mail is stored and forwarded to others. Newsgroups operate more like libraries. Email from conferences is sent not to individuals across the Internet but to electronic libraries of email stored on centrally located hard drives. These hard drives are often the storage systems of the user's Internet service provider. Rather than looking in a user's own private email box, an individual instead moves electronically to the library to call up the latest additions to the conference. If you are not sure whether you have a newsfeed to newsgroups, check with your Internet service provider. If you do not have a newsfeed, some sites provide direct Web access to newsgroup archives.

Mailing lists, often referred to as *listservs*, operate more like magazines delivered through the post office. Email is sent to all those who have subscribed to the conference. That is, you must send your email address to the "list" of email addresses of participants in the conference. Your addition to the list is done automatically by software. Once your name is on the list, any message sent to the conference will also be sent to you. You check your own personal email account to receive the latest messages from the conference.

## Newsgroup Examples

By searching for a newsgroup conference, you can find an individual who is interested in trading ideas on a selected topic. Another approach is to find a conference or group of people that frequently uses email to "talk about" or trade ideas on the topic in which you have an interest.

One of the simplest systems to search for newsgroups is CyberFiber's design (http://www.cyberfiber.com/). CyberFiber has cataloged thousands of newsgroups into different categories. Hunters can browse these subdivisions for conferences that may reference a certain topic. Searchers may also search either the title or description of the conferences. If you enter more than one search term, click a button to indicate whether the search is an AND search or an OR search. At present, these two forms of Boolean are all that CyberFiber offers.

If your browser is properly configured to find your service provider's newsfeed, Cyber-Fiber makes the link to the newgroup's email automatically. Otherwise no email will appear as CyberFiber does not provide a newsfeed.

# Searching Deja News for Newsgroups

## http://www.dejanews.com/

The DejaNews site provides a sophisticated search service, including full Boolean with parentheses.

By default, though, DejaNews uses AND in searches for email in any conference (forums). If you type in

```
cats dogs
```

you will receive only the email messages that focus on the topics of cats AND dogs. However, if you use OR you will receive conferences that cover *either* biology OR golf. You can click on the email messages to read them.

DejaNews provides four ways to reach newsgroups. The Browse Groups link lists progressive newsgroup hierarchies. Starting from a few top categories, each link takes you deeper into the outline of sub-categories. Eventually, you reach the email for a specific group. The Interest Finder option allows you to search for the newsgroup that uses your search term(s) most often. The result of the Interest Finder search lists newsgroups in rank order of their interest in your topic. The home page also lists newgroups by general categories called *Channels*. The fourth method and the default search on their home page is to search all of the email of all of the thousands of newsgroups for messages containing your search terms. It is hard to find a term that someone is not using in a newsgroup email message.

Though whichever of these four methods you reach, you can post a reply to the newsgroup at any time. Unlike some newsgroup search systems, your Web browser does not have to be configured to a local feed. Instead, DejaNews provides everything. Though the standard searches search databases of messages primarily between adults, a more specific adult heading is available from a quick pull-down menu next to the search field. Parents and educators will need to steer students away from this "adults only" collection of email conferences.

DejaNews also supports full Boolean in every field for data entry. To include phrases in your search, place them in quotation marks. Also, every left parenthesis must have a right parenthesis and vice versa. For example, you may want to find people who have discussed middle-level or junior high school books that have won awards, but not Dr. Seuss books or picture books. The DejaNews database would process a search strategy like this:

((honors OR awards) AND ("children's books")) NOT ("Dr. Seuss" OR Caldecott)

How many did you find? _____

Caldecott awards are prestigious awards, but they are for picture books more appropriate for younger readers. In this particular instance, DejaNews found 17 email messages matching this search strategy. When specialized searches do not work, use more general terms. A search using the Interest Finder link returns specific email conferences (forums).

"children's books"

How many did you find? _____

From *Decision Points: Boolean Logic for Computer Users and Beginning Online Searchers.*
© 1999 Libraries Unlimited, Inc. (800) 237-6124

found 11 forums. The highest ranked choice was "rec.arts.books.childrens," which discusses all aspects of children's literature. (Note: Newsgroups can be deleted and added, so at the time you try this search the results may be none or many newsgroups that match.)

## Liszt Newsgroups

Another Web company, Liszt (http://www.liszt.com/news/), offers newsgroup searching. Though full Boolean with parentheses cannot be entered in the search field, a pull-down menu nearby provides three options. The choice "all these words" is an AND search. The choice "any of these words" puts an OR between your search terms. The "exact phrase" choice treats your terms as one large word.

The search strategy of "children's books" returned only one newsgroup, "rec.arts. books.children's." When a newsgroup is found, users may use their local feed to read the e-mail, or use Liszt's online archives.

## Mailing Lists or Listservs

While newsgroup messages stay on a server until you request them, mailing list messages go straight to your email account. Users must be cautious in joining mailing lists. A single active list could add more than 300 email messages a week to your email account! It is important to carefully store the directions on how to take your name off the mailing list, in case the traffic becomes overwhelming. "Unsubscribe" is the most common command used to do this. On the whole, listservs generally offer a more academic orientation to their discussions than do newsgroups.

At the Liszt site (http://www.liszt.com/help.html), the full Boolean search strategies not available in hunting for Liszt's newsgroups can be used to find listserv email messages about award-winning juvenile literature. But they cannot be entered from the default home page. Instead, click the Search Help link. From the Search Help page, take the link to Advanced Searching. Here you can enter complex Boolean:

> ((honors OR awards) AND ("juvenile literature" OR children book)) NOT ("Dr. Seuss" OR Caldecott)

No matches were returned at the time of this writing.

The search was done again with the more general terms "children's books." This search found two matches: the Cherry-Valley-News Newsletter mailing list, which announces and reviews children's books, and NCCBA, a bookseller association.

What you cannot do with listservs, however, is search the email collection of thousands of electronic conferences with one search. This is possible with the newsgroup system, as DejaNews demonstrates. Because some listservs do archive their email, it is possible to subscribe and then search. Once you have subscribed, you have permission to search available archives. You can unsubscribe to any listserv and then subscribe again as often as you want. The process is handled automatically by software. However, because you must do this one archive at a time, the process will be tedious if you wish to examine the archives of many such conferences.

Several ways have now been introduced that use Boolean logic with different Internet systems for the purpose of interacting with people. The purpose of this people hunt is to reach the source that brings the greatest potential judgment to bear on a problem or question of interest, the human brain.

Though very valuable, it is important also to keep in mind the shortcomings of this level of the information pyramid. The types of people needed may not be found. If found, they may not have sufficient expertise. They may not be able or willing to respond in a time frame that meets your needs. The first answer returned may be questionable, and others who can check or validate that answer may not be available. Determining the quality of an answer is not trivial. For example, incorrect medical advice could be fatal. Incorrect legal advice could land you in jail.

These problems are best solved by different systems of information. People may have already put answers to questions in another system of information that you can examine. The information in this new location may also be used to check the answer given in an email conference. Furthermore, these places provide a menu of their immense resources that is visible over the Internet.

# Chapter 10

# Person, Place, or Thing

## Introduction

When explorers search the Internet for information stored in the physical world of libraries and museums, the exercise resembles a treasure hunt with many decision points. This hunt involves several stages of effort. The first decisions have to do with the "place" of the hunt. The treasure hunter must decide on the location in which the hunt for a "treasure map" will take place. Next, searches are conducted to find a map of the collection with clues to the location of the treasure chest. If the right clues are found, a decision must be made as to whether the hunter or someone else will be sent to bring the treasure home. When this information treasure chest finally arrives, one last set of decisions must still be made: Is there enough treasure, or do you need to go after more? After all, the chest of information may contain nothing of use or be only partially full. You will not know for sure until the chest has arrived.

In practice, this often means that the information-age hunter must have sufficient knowledge of geography to know the city and state in which a library is located. Once known, Internet tools allow the researcher to check the library's card catalog to see if the "treasure" book exists. If and when the hunter identifies a likely book, the search system responds with a book ID or call number, which serves as a clue to tell where this treasure is located. This call number allows the searcher to use the map of the library. Now anyone can move to the first floor, second shelf, and pull the third book from the left. Ultimately, finding a resource in this middle layer of the information pyramid means finding something on a shelf.

The next decision can involve considerable effort. Who will make the trip? If the library or bookstore is thousands of miles away, the hunter may decide to find an information "travel agent" to arrange a trip for this book or resource. At your local library, this travel system is known as *interlibrary loan*. If you searched a bookstore, your bookstore travel agent might use an overnight shipping agent such as FedEx or UPS. The Internet can be thought of as a virtual telescope through which you can "see" inside "places" on the Internet. Libraries, bookstores, museums, and other institutions make catalogs or databases of books, journals, magazines, broadcasts, exhibits, videotapes, and audiotapes visible over the Internet. At this level this telescope has strict limitations. You can "see" that a work is present but cannot see its contents. Until you receive and read the book, its value remains uncertain.

## Physical Libraries

There is a tendency among beginners, as well as among those more experienced with the Internet, to skip library-type searches and search for the fast and convenient Web page. (The process for Web page hunting is discussed in the next section.) As is noted there, "fast and convenient" is often a delusion. Hours can easily be lost in a vain hunt for data you are sure must be on the Web—somewhere.

In spite of the number of steps involved, the physical library has significant advantages over electronic databases and other information systems on the Internet. Works stored in libraries, museums, and bookstores, like networks of netheads (frequent users of online systems), represent another important cultural layer of human judgment. Significant judgment was used just to bring these collections together.

Although online systems generally provide some degree of online help files, the difference comes in the next level of support. In a library there is always a human being available during regular working hours to whom you can talk about a collection's content, its search features, and search strategy. At best, online systems of Web pages and other types of computer files provide only email support for questions. Also, information in physical libraries does not decay very rapidly. Though bookstores may sell out of a book, they know how to get another copy. Library collections have an even longer shelf life. If you find a resource listed in a card catalog, it is highly likely that the book will be in the library not only next week, but also 50 or 100 years from now. With computer files on the Internet, files that you find one moment may be erased the next. Your knowledge of their location has a kind of 180-day information half-life. *Half-life* in this context refers to the length of time that passes before half of your bookmarks to Internet files no longer function.

Another advantage is that library publications are generally longer and treat their topics more thoroughly than the average Web page. Most importantly, works published in libraries have generally received far more editing and revision at the hands of critical reviewers than the majority of computer files scattered across the Internet. There will come a moment in history when this difference is gone, but it will not arrive for some time yet.

Many public libraries do not make it easy to search just the collection of books useful to a wide range of public school student reading needs, but at least some make it possible. Bookstores and other systems already provide excellent service in this area. In contrast, it is impossible at present to search current Web and other Internet databases of computer files by the readability needs of various grade and age levels.

## Where to Search

When dealing with the "Place" issue and information stored as physical items, it is best to begin with a key question: Which place do you search first? To answer this you must first think geographically. Increasingly, public schools, city libraries, and bookstores have their "card" catalogs in digital format. It appears likely that all such institutions will eventually make their card catalogs available over the Internet; many do already. Begin with a convenient "closest to home" search strategy. For example, first search the library that is physically closest to you, perhaps the one down the hall or across the street. Then look outward in ever-larger circles. Is there a major library in a large metropolitan region within an hour's drive of your home? Use the Internet to search there next. However, instead of seeking the help of interlibrary loan services, consider making a personal visit. If you find that you need to make such trips frequently, get a membership card in that library so that you can check items out of its holdings.

For the most comprehensive searches, learn how to search the very largest and finest libraries: the large city libraries in the United States, such as Boston's or New York's; the largest university libraries, such as Harvard's; and the largest federal government library, the Library of Congress. In this increasingly global age, you may also need to find someone with skills in another language. There are hundreds of excellent libraries available in other countries, each with its own unique treasures.

Though there are thousands of online libraries, learning to use each one does not require learning a different system of Boolean logic. If you know how to search one library, you can use the same search software for hundreds of other libraries. However, if a library is large enough, it may hire its own programmers to create its own special search system. There will always be a few libraries whose search systems are unique to their operations. These systems will naturally take longer to learn, but they may offer a wider range of features through which to search the collections.

There is another interesting feature of this situation. Many libraries now have at least two different online search systems. The older system has generally been around for many years and has been heavily used by librarians and experienced library patrons. Though it usually has many complex Boolean features, it is not widely used. As Web pages came along, programmers simplified the work of searching. In many cases, though, this simplification in data entry also reduced the number of features made available to the public. Consequently, if you search a library from a Web page and do not find what you expect to find, there may be another way. Look for links on the library's Web page to find older search systems. If its Web pages do not show such a system, find a way to contact its reference librarians. Ask if there is another search system to which you may have access. Older often does not mean a weaker system, just a more complex and more powerful one that will require a little longer to learn. The Library of Congress (http://lcweb.loc.gov/catalog/) is a perfect example of these types of parallel systems. Their older, but more sophisticated, system is called LOCIS (Library of Congress Information System, the original mainframe-based retrieval system). LOCIS (telnet://locis.loc.gov) requires that you use a Telnet application to reach it. Telnet is an older text-oriented system for navigating the Internet. The Library of Congress also provides three Web-page-based search methods: word, browse, and experimental. This experimental system is integrating multimedia computer files with its records, so the results may not match those of the other systems.

One quick approach to finding any online library is to find the closest library with an Internet-accessible site. This might require a telephone call to your local librarian. It is common for library Web sites to provide starter lists of other online libraries.

## How Do You Find Sets of Online Libraries Using the Same Search Software?

Fortunately, there is more than one way to identify the groups of online libraries that use the same search software. One approach is to find the home Web page of the company that sells the search software. The Web site Yahoo! keeps a list of library vendors:

> http://www.yahoo.com/Business_and_Economy/Companies/
> Information/Library_Services/Software/

A second approach that appears useful is not as powerful as you might expect. Do not be misled by lists of libraries provided online by any given library. Though this is likely to be an excellent and useful list, it is not yet common for a library to identify which libraries use the same search software as the one you are visiting. Instead, they list libraries deemed of some value; these may well use a variety of different search software systems. The third approach is to use Scott and Macdonald's Webcat site, which provides a thorough list of the search software vendors and also displays a comprehensive set of links to the libraries that use each vendor's software:

http://library.usask.ca/hywebcat/vendors.html

New indexes of online libraries will continue to appear in many places on the Internet. Use some of these search terms with online Web search engines to help you find other collections of libraries: OPACs (online public access libraries), online library, library index, catalog of libraries. OPACs are easy to find and are an important resource in helping more mature readers and adults find the information they need. In spite of their visibility on the Internet, these college and university places are generally good hunting grounds only for the most capable readers. Those seeking books and related resources geared more toward students in grades K–12, especially elementary and middle-level students, need to look elsewhere.

## Books and Resources for K–12

Tools for finding resources for students are useful not only for students, but for parents and educators as well. Information hunters should look among the places that take special interest in what many libraries call juvenile literature: city and school libraries, commercial bookstores, and the Library of Congress.

### City Libraries

Most city libraries have made children's collections one of their specialties. City libraries often house large collections of works in special children's rooms and teen rooms. Most city libraries have also put their entire catalogs online. Once you have electronically browsed your local city library's collection, make an electronic field trip to the collections of such works in large metropolitan regions. The two largest in North America are in Boston and New York, but large city and regional libraries can be found in every state.

In spite of the high quality of their children's collections, many city libraries pose a common problem for electronic hunters: It is difficult to search children's works separate from the adult collection. Two examples appear typical. The Berkeley (California) Public Library's Web pages report a children's collection in the central library of more than 50,000 titles. The Boston (Massachusetts) Public Library's Web pages indicate a central library children's collection of more than 60,000 titles. However, even the library Web pages dedicated to the interests of children and adolescents do not describe how to search their age-level collections. In each case, the online cataloging system does not have a search term that can be used to hunt just within this collection. This is also a problem for many academic libraries at colleges and universities, even those with teacher education programs. These libraries could create special fields in their databases for children's and teenagers' books, but often lack the cataloging resources to make this happen. Searches must instead be based on subject headings, so adults' books become mixed with juvenile literature. The hunter (whether child or adult) must read through dozens of descriptions of books that are not relevant to the target age level.

With each city library, you will have to try some different approaches. If you become stumped, look for the email address of the library in question. Use email to ask the library staff if they know a special search strategy that will work. As a general rule, try searching the keyword or subject field for *children's books* or *juvenile literature*. If you search for *children's literature*, you may find works written by adults that review and discuss books created for children and adolescents. Some systems require you to search in the standard way for title or subject headings. Once this set is found, a "limit" command may be available to reduce the set for that search just to children's books.

# Cleveland Library:
## Searching a Public Library

http://www.cpl.org/

The Cleveland Public Library in Ohio has been one of the nation's leaders in online community access to library resources. Its cataloging software is provided by DRA (Data Research Associates). Its catalog page allows you to search by subject, author, and title and to limit these searches by materials, language, and publication date. It also provides keyword searching using many Boolean features: AND, OR, NOT, and parentheses. Further qualifier terms are available to force a keyword search of a particular field: au (author), ti (title), su (subject), nt (notes), pu (publisher). Its catalogers use several terms to identify works for preschool and K–12. However, they also add the term "juvenile literature" to the given subject heading of areas often used by children and adolescents, such as "history" or "animals." When such a work is actually written for children, the subject heading would look like this: Astronomy—juvenile literature.

From the home page, click on the link to the Catalog. Results will vary from the counts given here. Record your own number of hits.

_____ juvenile literature

Select the subject option. Enter this phrase in the search box. In the test search, the system responded with only one hit and a note to use the phrase "children's literature" instead.

_____ su juvenile literature

Select the keyword option. Enter this phrase in the search box. The system found 460,702 records in our test.

_____ children's stories

Select the subject option. Enter this phrase in the search box. The system found 944 titles in the test. It also listed other words to be used for related works; e.g., "fairy tales," which has 3,352 titles.

---

## Boolean:

_____ su juvenile literature AND dinosaurs

Select the keyword option. Enter this phrase in the search box. The system found 527 titles in the test.

_____ dogs or cats

Select the subject option. Enter this phrase in the search box. The system found no records.

_____ (dogs OR cats) NOT (ti puppies OR ti kittens)

Select the keyword option. Enter the above phrase in the search box. In our test the system found 7,775 records or hits.

Create some other search strategies and record the number of hits for each.

**Number of Hits**          **Search Strategy**

_____          _____

_____          _____

# Online Activity #3

# *Canton Public Library: Searching a Public Library with III*

http://www.metronet.lib.mi.us/CANT/homepage.html

The Canton Public Library in Michigan uses Innovative Interfaces, Inc. (III), to provide the library's searchable catalog software. Users can search by author, title, author/title (author AND title), subject, and words in the title series or contents. Only the word search allows the user to enter Boolean phrases using OR, AND, and parentheses. Boolean AND can also be done with other search categories using the "limit" command. The term *juvenile literature* is added to the subject heading of areas often used by children and adolescents, such as "history" or "animals." When such a work is actually written for children, the subject heading would look like this: Astronomy—juvenile literature. Search help information is provided on the search entry pages.

From the home page, click on the link to the Catalog page. Select the type of search you need. Record your number of hits.

_____ juvenile literature

Select the word (keyword) search option. Enter the above phrase in the search box. When tested, the system responded with only one hit, which had to do with juvenile reform and penal institutions. Select a subject search. In the test, no references were found, but a link was provided to the children's literature heading.

_____ children's literature

Select the subject search. Enter the above phrase in the search box. The system yielded 55 hits in this test search; however, the works were not for children but for adults reflecting on children's literature.

_____ children's stories

Select the word search. Enter the above phrase in the search box. A test called up 28 entries. Keyword searching in this system treats this phrase as an AND search of two words, children AND stories. With a subject search, it yielded 594 entries.

_____ animals—juvenile literature

Select a subject search. Enter the above phrase in the search box. The system found 46 titles in the test search.

---

## Boolean:

_____ dogs OR cats

Select the word (keyword) search option. Enter the above phrase in the search box. The system found 474 titles in the test search.

_____ dogs cats dogs AND cats

Select the word (keyword) search option. Enter each of the above phrases in the search box. The system found the same 20 titles in the test search for dogs and cats whether AND was included or not.

_____ (children's stories) and animals

You cannot enter the search strategy in this way using word search, but you can follow steps that have the same effect. First, do a subject search for children's stories, which returns 590 entries. Next, select the Limit Search option. From this screen, select Subject search. Enter the word animals. In a test, the system responded with 16 entries that were about animals and also in the category of children's stories.

Based on your interests, record some strategies of your own and the number of resources (hits) found.

**Number of Hits**       **Search Strategy**

_____         _____

_____         _____

_____         _____

# *The Public Library of Nashville and Davidson County: Another Example of Public Library Searching*

## http://waldo.nashv.lib.tn.us/

The Public Library of Nashville and Davidson County (Tennessee) uses Innovative Interfaces, Inc. (III) to provide the library's searchable catalog software. Users can search by author/illustrator, title/series, subject, and call number. Boolean AND can be done with these search categories using the "limit" command. A keyword search allows the user to enter Boolean phrases. The Boolean terms include OR, AND, NO or NOT, parentheses, and truncation using "*". The term *juvenile literature* is added to the subject heading of areas often used by children and adolescents, such as "history" or "animals." When such a work is actually written for children, the subject heading would look like this: Astronomy—juvenile literature.

From the home page, click on the link to the Catalog page. Select the type of search needed. Record your own number of hits. Results will vary over time.

_____ juvenile literature

Select the "key words" search option. Enter the search in the search box. The system responded with 20,688 titles.

_____ children's literature

Select the subject search. Enter this phrase in the search box. The system found 755 items in the test search; however, the works are not for children, but rather written by and for adults reflecting on children's literature.

_____ animals

Using this phrase with a keyword search, a test resulted in 4,049 entries.

---

## Boolean:

_____ animals AND (juvenile literature)

Select a keyword search. Enter this phrase in the search box. The system found 1,135 items in the test search.

_____ dogs OR cats

Select the word (keyword) search option. Enter this phrase in the search box. The system found 2,507 items in the test search.

_____ children's stories and animals

Select the word (keyword) search option. Enter the above phrase. The system found 62 entries.

_____ (children's stories) and animals

Using a subject search, you cannot enter the search strategy in this way, but you can follow steps that have the same effect. First, do a subject search for children's stories, which returns 1,205 entries. Next, select the Limit Search option. From this screen, select Subject search. Enter the word animals. In the test, the system then responded with 29 entries that were about animals and also were in the category of children's stories.

_____ (toys AND batteries) OR (computers AND games) NOT magnet

Select the keyword search. Enter the above phrase. Our test returned 13 hits.

_____ automobile

Using the above term, select the keyword search. Our test returned 684 hits.

_____ auto*

Using the above characters, select the keyword search. Our test returned 2,503 items.

Based on your interests, write and then test some search strategies of your own. Record your number of hits.

**Number of Hits**          **Search Strategy**

_____          _____

_____          _____

_____          _____

## Bookstores

Many bookstores are putting their own store catalogs on the Internet. Others take advantage of the Internet to dispense with the storefront altogether; they use only a warehouse and ordering staff, with all sales occurring via the electronic universe. Their databases also list videos, audiobooks, CD-ROMs, and music CDs. One can expect that digital video disc (DVD) titles will be appearing soon as well. The databases also include books in languages other than English. Increasingly, these online stores are providing special search windows for the selection of children's books and related resources. The number of businesses offering this service and the manner in which their services operate will undoubtedly change rapidly. Currently, 2Million Books, Barnes & Noble, and Amazon are three of the largest online bookstore services. Of note is the fact that each of these businesses provides a special feature for the searching of children's books. Each of them has approached the problem in unique but useful ways.

This is in contrast to public and academic libraries. The bookstores have more tags for juvenile literature, though they do not use that term. For example, in public and academic libraries you may sometimes find children's books under *juvenile literature* and at other times under *children's stories* or other subject headings. Bookstores have broken out the category of juvenile literature into many useful subcategories. Depending on the bookstore this might include preschool, children, and adolescents, or specified age-level categories. Also, these bookstores highlight the path to children's resources on their home pages and provide more detailed help information with the search procedure. In general, the number of useable Boolean features is much greater and more clearly highlighted for use.

### Barnes & Noble

#### http://barnesandnoble.com/

The Barnes and Noble home page has used different terms for children's interests over the years, from children to kids. When you find and click on this link, a search area appears for juvenile literature. They use five age categories: young adult, 9 through 12, 7 and 8, 4 through 6, and infant and preschool. From their home page, click the word *Children* at the top of the page. Descriptions of best-selling children's books fill this page.

### Amazon

#### http://www.Amazon.com

At this writing, Amazon provides the greatest flexibility for searching. From its home page, click on the Search button. One can use the main search page to find children's books, but there is a simplified page exclusively for children and young adult publications. This page reveals three useful options. It provides a link to advice on searching. It provides a link to children and to young adult categories and separates each into its own pages. Each of the two category pages includes numerous descriptions of current best-selling titles. The children's page has 19 categories and the young adult page provides 13. The children-young adult search page itself is the third option.

The children-young adult page sets up an AND search using a combination of keywords and age ranges. It provides buttons for the same four sets of age ranges as does 2Million Books: baby through preschool, ages 4 through 8, ages 9 through 12, and young adult. The user clicks on one of these four buttons to indicate age range for the search. The user must also place terms in a keyword field. You can search any combination of age ranges by clicking more than one age-range button. To search all age ranges, click all of the buttons or none of them.

From this search page, it is especially useful to take the link to Children's and Young Adults' Search Tips and read the advice. In the single entry box for placing keywords, you can enter multiple author terms or multiple title or subject terms, but in this quick search format you cannot search both the title and subject categories at the same time. The system must automatically pick one set in the database or the other. If you enter an author's name and then a term from a title, it will search either the author category or the title and subject categories in the database, but it will not do both. To search for an author, you could use **Houston** or **Gloria Houston**. To search for concepts you could enter **art** and **nature**. The search will retrieve all works that match *all* the terms you enter, meaning that it does an AND search using all terms.

Doing an AND search with multiple categories requires use of the main search page. You can still search the four age ranges from this page, but you must precisely enter these long sets of characters in the subject field: **child books/baby-preschool, child books/ages 4-8, child books/ages 9-12, or child books/young adult**. Other terms can be added to the subject field as well, separated by spaces. However, not all books have data entered in the subject field and many books are indexed by multiple subject terms. Further, the author and keyword category boxes can be searched simultaneously. Your search will retrieve all works that match all of your entries, meaning that it does an AND search using all terms.

If these options are not enough, Amazon also provides a Power Search Web page with detailed instructions for its use. You can search these fields: title, title word, subject, subject word, author, keyword, ISBN, and publication date (pdate). Along with the Boolean values of AND, OR, and NOT, the search system allows the use of many other terms: equals, greater, during, is, less, between, isn't, greater or equal, before, starts, less or equal, after, begins, higher, earlier, lower, and later. You can use parentheses to group terms, which allows a more precise statement of your search.

When using Power Search, put double quotes ("") around phrases, especially those using Boolean terms that might be interpreted as a special search command. If you search the title category for the phrase **"Eagle or Sun"** with quotation marks around it, and then search with the same phrase without the quotation marks, you will get very different results. With the quotation marks, the system looks for just that precise arrangement of letters. This search found five such titles. Without the quotation marks, the search will find both books about eagles plus books about the sun. This second search strategy found several hundred titles.

### Acses

**http://www.acses.com**

Acses is a comparison shopper Web site. Its specialty is comparing the prices of books from more than 25 online bookstores. You can search four different categories of information: title, author, keyword, and ISBN. It currently offers very basic Boolean features: AND and OR. So, after you've used more powerful Boolean and special categories at other online book sites, enter your book information at Acses to find the best price.

### K–12 Options

In summary, Amazon provides a full range of search options. At the easiest level, it provides a page of categories from which to select. For more complex work, it provides powerful form completion pages. Its most powerful method allows long sentences of search terms and values. Barnes & Noble also has an easy-to-use system for the selection of children's publications. As each of these systems returns a precise overall count of the number of books found, it is possible to make comparisons about the thoroughness of each bookstore. You can use Acses to make a thorough comparison of price.

 *Activity #5*

# *Searching Amazon Bookstore*

### http://www.amazon.com/

Amazon Bookstore is an online service only. There is no physical storefront in the standard sense. Search help information is provided on a number of pages. Searching for children's resources is well defined. Amazon also provides a Power Search Web page with detailed instructions for its use. You can search these fields: title, title word, subject, subject word, author, keyword, ISBN, and publication date (pdate). Along with the Boolean values of AND, OR, and NOT, the search system allows the use of many other terms: equals, greater, during, is, less, between, isn't, greater or equal, before, starts, less or equal, after, begins, higher, earlier, lower, and later. You can use parentheses to group terms. Quotation marks ("") are used around phrases.

From Amazon's home page, click on the link at the top of the page. Along the left edge, select "Children's Books by Age."

Select the age range 9–12 by clicking on the square in front of that age. This will place an X in the choice box. Record your own number of hits. Results will vary over time.

---

## Boolean:

_____ dogs cats

Enter this phrase in the search box. This is treated as an AND search. The system found 24 titles for 9-to 12-year-olds in our test.

_____ title word is "logic" and "circuit" and "teachers"

Select the Power Search link and enter this phrase. The system found one entry.

_____ (subject is "cats" or "dogs") and (subject is "child books/ages 9-12" and "published after 1997")

You cannot do OR searches from the basic keyword search screen. Instead, select the Power Search link and enter this phrase in the Power Search box. This allows an OR search. The system found 23 titles.

_____ (subject is animals) and (subject is "child books/ages 9-12" and published after 1997)

Select the Power Search link. Enter this phrase in the Power Search box. The system found 15 entries.

_____ subject is animals and "child books/baby-preschool" and published after 1997

Select the Power Search link. Enter this phrase in the Power Search box. The system found 19 entries.

_____ title word is rhyming and subject is "child books/baby-preschool" and published after 1993

Select the Power Search link and enter this phrase. The system found two entries.

From *Decision Points: Boolean Logic for Computer Users and Beginning Online Searchers.*
© 1999 Libraries Unlimited, Inc. (800) 237-6124

_____ (author is Isaac Asimov and subject is not "science fiction" and published after 1995)

Select the Power Search link and enter this phrase. The system found 37 entries.

Based on your interests, write and then test some search strategies of your own. Record your number of hits.

**Number of Hits**          **Search Strategy**

_____          _____

_____          _____

_____          _____

## Elementary, Middle, and High School Libraries

The newest way to use your Boolean skills to find qualified collections of children's readings is to search school district libraries. Searching bookstores basically tells you what the publishers have to sell. Searching school libraries tells you what districts have rated as useful enough to keep on hand. Because schools are already divided into elementary, middle, and high school levels, these children and young adult collections come presorted by age level. This exciting development greatly focuses the searching process. This feature is not yet common, but will become increasingly so in the next couple of years. Now you can begin to search K–12 libraries across the Internet. In the not-too-distant future, you will be searching the libraries in your local school buildings from your desktop.

There are two reasons for this rapid change. School buildings are in an accelerated development phase of wiring schools and classrooms for direct, high-speed Internet access. This process replaces the common arrangement of a single computer, with telephone line and slow modem, with direct Internet access for every computer in the building. Teachers will be able to have students search the building's library without leaving the classroom. This wiring infrastructure changeover is sweeping the country. Second, at the same time, libraries are getting the software they need to go online. Two of the major providers of school library automation software, Follett and Winnebago, are adding the features needed to their software for school librarians to make collections visible over the Internet. Follett reports that its company's software has a "presence in nearly 40,000 schools and libraries in more than 65 countries." Its Internet-accessible software became available as of January 1998. It will, of course, take some time for schools to upgrade to the Internet-accessible version; only a tiny fraction of Follett systems currently have their catalogs available online. Winnebago, reporting more than 25,000 schools using its software, is promising Internet accessibility for its software in the fourth quarter of 1998. Other vendors are also making similar upgrades to their software.

### *Follett's Sample Sites*

**http://www.ourlibrary.com**

Follett's software has three major screens: the startup; search a single category; and search up to three categories using Boolean AND, OR, and NOT. Graphic symbols accompany text describing the function of different search buttons on each screen.

The opening screen provides a single line for the entry of a search term. There is no indication whether it is searching one field in particular or all fields for the term you enter. There is no indication of whether it can handle more than one term. You simply have to have enough experience with the system to know what it expects on this first screen. Click on a category button in the menu bar depending on what kind of search you need: keyword, title, author, subject, series, or call number.

The system responds with a second screen displaying a keyword search and a list of publications in alphabetical order by keyword. This second screen allows you to further refine the search by making choices from among different category buttons on a menu bar at the top of the Follett window. These choices include keyword, title, author, subject, call number, and series title. The original search term is left displayed on the screen. Clicking among these alphabetical choices uses that same term to search a new category. In each case the term is displayed in its place in an alphabetical listing of terms. If the item is not found, the alphabetical list is still displayed, but with those terms that come after the point in the alphabet at which the term would have appeared had it been on the list. The search term or terms can be changed at any time. Each of the alphabetical lists contains links and symbols that can be clicked to show more detail about the selected publication.

This single-category search screen also has other important buttons. The Help button provides a basic review of all buttons. There is also a Power Search button, which allows the use of Boolean terms. If your search with simpler screens produces too many titles, you can use the Power Search screen to reduce the number you receive. As you have learned so far, you can use Boolean logic to remove titles that are less relevant to your needs.

# Follett Incorporated

http://www.ourlibrary.com/

The school cataloging software company called Follett provides a feature that allows school library catalogs to be searched by those outside the school building, using the Internet. Having arrived at the Follett Web address, take the link to "Follett School Library." On the next screen, take the link to "Search the Library."

_____ tree

Enter this word in the opening quicksearch screen entry box. The system completed a keyword search and found 12 items in the test search.

_____ tree

When the menu bar screen appears, click the title button. If the word *tree* is found in the list of titles, it is displayed in alphabetical order along with other books that do not have *tree* in the title. Because this is an alphabetical listing, there may also be works with *tree* in the title on the previous screen. Click the "Prev" (previous) button to check. If *tree* does not appear, a list of books will still be selected. At the top of this list will be the next word in the collection after the word *tree*. The same positioning in an alphabetical list is also used for author and subject searching.

_____ tree

Click the Power button, which is a magnifying glass. From the pull-down menu after the field in which *tree* has already been entered, select "All." All categories are searched for items containing the word *tree*.

_____ author=Houston and title=Arizona not subject=state

You cannot enter a search in this manner, but you can enter terms in three separate entry boxes. Use the pull-down menu to select the term that matches this search strategy. Click the radio buttons (round circles) to select relevant Boolean logic.

The Power Search screen provides three distinct boxes or places for the entry of search terms. Enter your search word in one or more of these boxes. A pull-down menu at each entry field enables the user to select which fields will be searched: All, Title, Author, Notes, Subject, and Series. Three radio buttons may then be clicked to indicate a Boolean value: AND, OR, and NOT. Next, use the pull-down menu to tell which part of the database's record should be searched.

## The Library of Congress

The catalog of the Library of Congress (LC) is a powerful tool that meets many search needs. By law, the LC must catalog all works published in this country. All children's titles, in and out of print, can be found there. The LC catalog gains its power from its immense size and the variety of its search systems. The LCWeb system (http://lcweb.loc.gov/catalog/) is relatively easy to search. The more powerful LOCIS system (telnet://locis.loc.gov) provides powerful Boolean options.

All information hunters will benefit from viewing a reference book found in nearly every library—the *Library of Congress Catalog*. This lists the words used to catalog its books. Works for preschoolers, children, and adolescents are described in this database as "juvenile literature." Search results vary depending on which of LC's four search methods you use. The word and browse methods apparently do not treat "juvenile literature" as a phrase. These systems reported that one of the search terms appeared too many times in the database for further processing. The experimental system (ESS) does process this as a phrase. ESS returned exactly 5,000 hits (citations) in a test search. The manual command method, also referred to as LOCIS, produced the most significant results.

LOCIS is really three different databases: (1) 1898 to 1949, (2) 1950 to 1974, and (3) 1975 to the present. Our test search, using the phrase "juvenile literature," showed the count of books as follows and in this way:

(1) B06+Juvenile literature//(SUBJ=122)
(2) B06+Juvenile literature//(SUBJ=10,421)
(3) B06+Juvenile literature//(SUBJ=53,979)

Adding up the numbers after the equal signs gives you the current total of the books cataloged under this subject heading in the LC. This means that a collection of more than 64,000 books for children can be searched from your desktop computer. It is possible then to do further AND searches on children's books with another LC subject term, such as *cats, fiction,* or *science.*

The preferred approach in LOCIS is not to type in one long phrase of Boolean ((cat OR kitten) AND health), but rather to do a search for each term individually. The results of each search are referred to as a *set*. These sets can be combined in different ways using Boolean terminology. To further reduce the search to books published after a certain year, LOCIS provides a "limit" command. To limit search set number 3 to just books published in 1991 or later, the user would type in this text:

limit 3/yri eg 1991

The 3 is the number of a previous search. There is a search history command (history) that will give you the numbers for those sets or searches.

# *Searching the Library of Congress—LOCIS*

### telnet://locis.loc.gov

To search the Library of Congress Information System (LOCIS), you need a common software application, a Telnet application. Telnet applications use and display only text. Text means just numbers and letters. Text travels faster than graphics and multimedia. It also takes up much less space on diskettes and hard drives. Because of these advantages, Telnet procedures will remain a speedy and useful way to zip through cyberspace in the years ahead.

Telnet applications were the means one used to travel the Internet before the more graphics-oriented Web and Gopher systems came into being. You may need to consult with a local computer expert to find the right Telnet application for your computer and operating system. This worksheet assumes that you are sitting at a computer that is connected to the Internet through a modem or some other method.

There are two common ways to start searching using Telnet commands. First, you can start with Internet software called Web browsers. These Web browsers, such as Netscape and Internet Explorer, can be configured to automatically start up a Telnet program when one is needed. Second, you can start with a program that knows how to do only Telnet commands.

The first method assumes that your Web browser is configured to know where your Telnet application is. The letters and numbers in the following example lines are the characters you need to type. After you type them, press the enter or return key. If you choose to use this method, enter this address in the location field (URL) at the top of your Web browser:

telnet:// locis.loc.gov

A second approach is to work directly from the Telnet application itself. Find and start your Telnet application. Next, open a Telnet connection to the address of:

locis.loc.gov

You will see how Boolean logic gets used in a moment. For now, follow these steps.

When you see the Telnet window titled LOCIS : LIBRARY OF CONGRESS INFORMATION SYSTEM, select: 1 Library of Congress Catalog. (Remember to always press the enter or return key after you have entered the required command.)

1

The following screen indicates that the Library of Congress divides its collections into three locations or databases by a range of dates. From the next screen select: 3 BOOKS cataloged since 1975 LOC3:

3

At the bottom of the next screen, type commands to browse for the topic of science in the subject field. The two hyphens force a search of the subject field:

b science--

From the next screen that is returned, select the sixth field, which holds the largest number of books found:

    s b6

Now type these commands and press the return key at the end of each line:

    b juvenile literature—

    s b6

    b mathematics—

    s b6

    H

The H command (search History) shows a list of all the entered searches.

---

***** SEARCH HISTORY ***** SETS 1 - 7 OF 7

| SET 1 | 49: | SLCT LOC3/TITL/Science |
| SET 2 | 11,728: | SLCT LOC3/SUBJ/Science |
| SET 3 | 11: | SLCT LOC3/SERI/Science |
| SET 4 | 53,979: | SLCT LOC3/SUBJ/Juvenile literature |
| SET 5 | 55: | SLCT LOC3/TITL/Mathematics |
| SET 6 | 7,582: | SLCT LOC3/SUBJ/Mathematics |
| SET 7 | 3: | SLCT LOC3/SERI/Mathematics |

---

Remember that all of these searches covered publications only from 1975 onward. Sets 1, 2, and 3 were the result of the selection of all science books (**b science--**). For example, set 2 shows that there are 11,728 books labeled with the subject of science. Set 4 was the result of the search for all works of juvenile literature (**b juvenile literature--**). Exactly 53,979 books were found. Sets 5, 6, and 7 were the result of the search for all works of mathematics (**b mathematics--**). Set 6, for example, shows that 7,582 works were found under the subject heading of mathematics.

Boolean logic is now needed to find just the books for students on the topic of science and mathematics. To do this, you combine the numbers from the sets using Boolean terms such as AND, OR, and NOT. This can be expressed in different ways.

AND statements must be written as follows:

    COMBINE 4 AND 2 (combines records from BOTH set 2 and set 4)

OR statements must be written as follows:

    COMB 2o6 (combines records from EITHER set 2 or set 6) This shortened form can also be entered as COMB 2 or 6.

NOT statements must be written as follows:

    C 2 NOT 6 (combines only records from set 2 that are not also in set 6)

The command to combine can be spelled out completely or abbreviated at any time to COMB or C.

Continue to enter the commands shown here. At the READY FOR NEW COMMAND prompt, type:

```
COMB 4 AND (2 or 6)
SET 8 667: COMB 4 AND (2 OR 6)
```

Set 8 found 667 works that met these Boolean conditions. The next command limits set 8 to publications cataloged in the year 1998 and beyond. That is, any publications dated before 1998 are removed, leaving only the most current books. At the READY FOR NEW COMMAND prompt, type:

```
L 8/yri eg 1998
SET 9 31: LIMIT 8/YRI EG 1998
```

The "limit" command acts as an additional AND search; that is, you tell the system to search through the 667 books of set 8 and retrieve only those books with a publication date of 1998 or later. This reduced the number of books to only 31. If at any time you wish to explore the contents of a set, use the display command, which can be reduced to simply the letter D. At the READY FOR NEW COMMAND prompt, type:

```
display set9
```

Once you have started to display items, use the following two-letter commands. They allow you to flip through the screen pages of the publications that you found:

NP (next page)
PP (previous page)
P# (specific page [e.g., P3])

To see more information on a certain book listed on the screen, type the number found in front of the book and press the enter or return key.

Type HELP for a list of further commands. For help on particular commands, type **HELP** and the command name (e.g., **HELP COMBINE**).

Now use these skills to experiment with your own Library of Congress search projects. For example, use these techniques to record below the number of books for students you can find on:

cats____ cars____ stars____

wolves____ trees____ Legos____

animals____ President Clinton____

---

## Reflection

It is important to reflect for a moment on that number of 64,000 books for students in the Library of Congress. This seems like a large number until one realizes that the LC database holds more than 27 million books. The implications are interesting if they are accurate. If the cataloging was comprehensive, in the last 100 years our country has produced just 0.002 percent of its books for younger readers! What this number may also indicate is that the LC's search system is not as comprehensive as hunters seeking juvenile literature might hope. This makes knowledge of other ways to search for children's books and resources a valuable skill. Both city libraries and bookstores that were discussed previously provide other sets of information systems that reflect these entities' particular interest in collecting and distributing resources for children and adolescents.

# Chapter 11

# Person, Place, or Thing

Your Person hunts led you to brains. Your Place hunt led you to shelves of books and perhaps other media. Now your Thing hunt will lead you to hard drives. When treasure hunters search for works stored in the virtual or electronic world of hard drives, the hunt can go much faster than a search in the physical world. This time, the clues that the Internet returns come with a map and a treasure attached by an electronic thread. One no longer has to make decisions about who will go get the identified items that need retrieving. To decide to use the clue is to have the computer network serve as your delivery agent. Clicking on the clue pulls the thread, which brings the treasure chest into your living room or office and opens it. When shifting from library searching to Web page searching, your thinking changes from searching for a place to searching for the real Thing.

## Virtual World Problems

There are some problems in the virtual world. Usually, to find the clue is to be able to make a decision on whether to open that treasure chest. Sometimes, though, the clue is no longer correct or accurate. Someone may have moved or erased the treasure or even changed it so that it does not match the clue. Pulling the electronic thread may result in fetching nothing or receiving something much different from what you expected.

The Internet can be used to bypass the question of "where" the information is kept. Search systems that identify *things* stored electronically on the Internet automatically know the answer to the question of location. The hunter must focus instead on finding the thing that is needed. This Thing is an electronic file containing the information you need. To find an electronic file on the Internet is to be able to have a copy of it. At this new level, the system moves a copy of the Thing you are after directly to your computer workstation. This is a subtle but important distinction over information transfer in the physical world; there the original is relocated, and thus it no longer exists in its first location. Because it is no longer in its original location, it is not as available to the next person who wants it. The Thing—information shaped as some form of media—clones itself to flow electronically from computer to computer. No matter how many people get the Thing, it is always available for the next person who wants it. These Things form the base of the information pyramid.

Electronic storage of data means that not only paper, but also audio and video in any form, need not be physically transferred from one geographic location to another, nor is another set of people needed to assist with this second step. Nor does acquisition require a third step of finding different technology to display the information, because the computer is capable of displaying all electronic media formats. To find a Thing on the Internet is almost the same as having it. The Internet can allow you to reach inside hardware on the Internet and move computer files stored there to your computer. These files might be text, still images, audio, animation, or video, or some combination of all of these in one screen display. These Things are found on hard drives that individuals or institutions are willing to make public. These computer files are stored and accessed through a variety of systems that have developed over the past few years, including the World Wide Web, Gopher networks, and File Transfer Protocol (FTP). A copy of the data moves straight from the place where the data is stored to your electronic workstation.

It now appears that you have far fewer decisions to make in the virtual world. A search and a click and you are there! Well … so much for appearances. In fact, after you have opened your electronic treasure chest, you have a set of decisions to make that have far greater consequences in the virtual world. To understand this, it is useful to return to the idea of human judgment. As different human beings reflected on and helped to review and change a work or publication, they added human judgment to that work. This raises the quality or value of the work. There is also greater incentive in the physical world to make sure that such value has been added. There is a real and significant cost in producing a work using a medium such as paper or plastic (audio, video, or compact disc) and those who take the risk want to make sure that they can sell what they have helped to create. These publishers put their potential publications or works through a series of quality checks.

When you receive your electronic Thing in the virtual world, you generally have no idea how much human judgment was added to it. It is possible that these ideas went directly from someone's mind to publication as a file placed on a hard drive, which, in turn, was connected to the Internet. Later the hunter's search finds this file. The hunter must now make many important decisions. Although these questions should be asked about any publication, they take on more importance in the virtual realm. Are the topics and imagery age-appropriate? Is the Thing biased or slanted in ways that must be explained to certain audiences (such as children)? Is its readability appropriate for the age in question? Is it well written? Is the information current? Is it truthful?

## The Hunt Across the Web

If the hunter in the virtual world prepares carefully, she can greatly improve the quality of what she captures. What is captured often depends on the tools with which one hunts. Currently it is possible to divide databases (e.g., search engines) of Internet files into four groups, based on the degree of human judgment involved in the collection of their contents. These search tools can also be thought of as another pyramid, a pyramid of four rooms of information. In the top room are resources that are of the highest quality—but this room contains the fewest specimens. As the hunter moves down the pyramid's levels, she enters rooms with ever-greater quantities of specimens with ever-greater variation in quality.

At the bottom level is an immense quantity—that is, attempts to index everything on the Internet. "Everything on the Internet" means all the files in all the Internet-accessible sections of all the hard drives on the planet. It contains everything found in the rooms above in addition to everything those layers do not have. This includes information that has not yet been found by reviewers and catalogers, either because it is too new or because they simply have not yet been able to find it. It also includes everything they rejected as being unworthy of review. Sometimes in this layer hunters grab something they hope is edible and find out later they were misled by a rock or by the label on some trash. Sometimes they find a wonderful specimen of information that they can drag back to their cook stoves. At this level, hunters must have a sharper eye for items that look like game but are just decoys, as well as for useful information that has been disguised by unusual coverings.

## The Top Level of the Web: Commercial Publications

Commercial online publications are generally full-text. That is, if you search and find a company's Web pages or database for an article or other work that is for sale, you can read the full or complete piece online at your computer. These publications may be from publishers who are already selling magazines, newspapers, and other works and who subsidize what appears on their Web pages with inserted advertisements. Often they put pieces of articles or even entire publications online for free. The company's reputation as a news and information organization is at stake, so the work is carefully edited and reviewed.

### Encyclopaedia Britannica

**http://www.eb.com/**

*Encyclopaedia Britannica* is an example of an online resource for which you must pay a monthly subscription fee. Searches of this encyclopedia retrieve the same well-reviewed and well-written articles that are in the paper encyclopedia. The electronic articles, however, also have Web page links to high-quality Internet sites that have been previewed for their accuracy and usefulness in relation to the encyclopedia article.

Many libraries have special online subscription rates to this resource. If a community's library does, any member of the community may search it free of charge, but they must be at the local library to do so, or have an online password provided by the library.

Other examples of commercial sites are listed at:

http://www.yahoo.com/Business_and_Economy/Companies/Information/

### Time-Warner's Pathfinder

**http://www.pathfinder.com/**

Time-Warner's Pathfinder site integrates articles and stories from Time-Warner's large family of magazine publications, such as *Fortune*, *Time*, and *Money*. It is not possible to tell which stories are just for online publication and which were taken (in whole or in part) from stories that appear in the newsstand publications. Whatever the case, a wide variety of issues and areas are well-covered and accessible free of charge.

Similar sites can be found at:

http://www.yahoo.com/Business_and_Economy/Companies/News_and_Media/

# The Second Level of the Web:
# Professionally Reviewed Internet Sites

Adults, adolescents, and children are already familiar with a wide range of commercially published magazines and books. It is often easy to tell just by the title of a source if its articles are age-appropriate. A commercial publisher's content is very much the same quality, whether on paper or on the Internet. But titles mean little when the source shifts from commercial publications to millions of Internet Web pages across tens of thousands of computer sites. Consequently, teachers, parents, and children have special review needs. Further, all users of the Internet have a need for sources that meet high standards for information access, including ease of use, accuracy, and timeliness of data. Organizations that provide such reviews will increasingly become the most valued resources on the Internet.

Educators' first priority must be safety. School zones in our neighborhoods use a variety of means to enable children and adolescents to grow and explore within the safety of their embrace. This embrace includes environments that are safe not only physically but also emotionally. The concerns are the same when it comes to the Internet. Safe zones have rules for contact with outsiders. Likewise, safe sites should not include sexually explicit or other inappropriate material (e.g., inappropriate language, graphic violence, drug use, gambling, discrimination, tastelessness, or instructions for universally criminal acts).

Most major search databases use software robots to automatically index the Internet in the most comprehensive manner possible. These databases are often called *search engines*. Their ideal is to have a reference to every public Internet file on the planet. However, anyone who owns a computer can become an Internet publisher in minutes. Some information creators choose to exercise their freedom of expression in ways that many find questionable. This work becomes caught up in the database of online resources. This data is then made generally available to whoever searches for certain words.

Children and adolescents need to learn to use information that is on the Internet. They need to learn the methods of Boolean logic that enable them to more effectively hunt in the forest of Web pages. American schools are in a position to make this happen; American schools are providing global leadership in putting classrooms online at an accelerated rate. But as teachers and families become educated to the power of search engines, they will also realize that they must take increasing care when using such tools.

The need for caution depends on the outcome of the current strategy. The current strategy is to buy software applications or systems that promise to screen and filter out sites whose nature would be a problem for children and schools. You could think of this expense as a kind of tax on children's resources that is necessary to keep the Internet suitable for their needs. When a search is under way, Web pages that might be accessed are checked against a list of inappropriate sites and pages. Only those not on a reserve list will be sent on to the student. To find such blocking and filtering software, you can study the list of such companies provided by Yahoo!:

http://www.yahoo.com/Business_and_Economy/Companies/Computers/
Software/Internet/Blocking_and_Filtering/Titles/

This blocking raises additional concerns about freedom of expression and First Amendment rights, but a more complete treatment of these issues is beyond the scope of this book. For sites from which to begin a more thorough examination of these concerns, investigate these pages:

Electronic Frontier Foundation   http://www.eff.org/blueribbon.html
Electronic Privacy Information Center (12/97)   http://www2.epic.org/reports/
filter_report.html
Parents Guide to the Internet   http://www.ed.gov/pubs/parents/internet

Another family-friendly strategy could also emerge: removal of unsuitable Web pages from the search engine itself. Any Web page link provided would thus automatically be appropriate for further use by students and classrooms. Nevertheless, once age-appropriate sites have been found, other issues arise which are common to any medium or type of information, such as readability, interest level, and accuracy.

These child and family issues highlight the value and importance of human judgment and the value of knowing which companies and corporations responsibly exercise the constitutional right of free speech. Consequently, it is valuable to be aware of companies that have made it their core business to review, annotate, and/or rate Internet Web sites. There are many that operate in a great variety of ways.

## Family Filter from Alta Vista

**http://www.altavista.com/**

The AltaVistaWeb site takes a distinctive but useful approach to the concept of review. Their screened reviewers, who constitute a representative sample of the online community, evaluate for family appropriateness. They use a democratic vote of the selected Net community members, who are not hired professional writers. Any use of this search engine yields only family-, school-, and child-safe sites scattered across the Internet. Through the use of a large number of these volunteer third-party evaluators and programming routines, Alta Vista seeks to evaluate most of the sites on the Internet.

AltaVista (AV) titles this feature the "AV Family Filter." When you first arrive at the AV site, this feature is not functioning. Any searches you conduct will not use the filter until it is activated. After you click the AV Family Filter link, you turn the filter on when you click the "Continue" or "Start AV Family Filter" button. AV also provides the option of making up a password which is then later required to turn off the filter. When the filter is active, a red plus sign appears in front of the "AV Family Filtered" link. Before beginning Online Activity #8, instructors should start up the filter for each computer workstation involved in the exercise. To determine both how much is removed by the filter and how much (in your judgment) should not have been removed by the filter, make the same search with the filter both on and off.

# *Searching from Alta Vista*

### http://www.altavista.com/

AltaVista provides a number of features for searching. Most of these options increase the user's ability to narrow the search. The plus (+) sign is used for AND and the minus (-) sign is used for NOT. Quotation marks should be placed around a phrase. There are nine commands for searching different parts of a Web page: **anchor** (the blue underlined words); **apple** class, **domain** name, **host** name, **image** filename, **link** URL, **text** not in the Web page's elements, **title** text, and **URL** text. In your search strategy enter the boldface word followed by a colon and the appropriate string of text. For example, TITLE: ANIMALS. The Advanced Search page provides a large window for entering longer Boolean phrases but the Help page does not explain whether this Boolean includes parentheses. The only place where you can expand your search using OR is in this larger Advanced Search window. The terms here are words you can use to practice searching this Web site. It *does* matter whether your word or words are uppercase or lowercase; the results will be different because this search engine is case-sensitive if upper-case is used. Lowercase retrieves any use of case. Record your own number of hits in the space provided.

---

## Single Word:

_____ cow

In the search box, enter a single word. The system retrieves any computer file in the database that contains that word. A number of items were found, but this system does not reveal the total number of items found by its searches.

---

## Phrase:

_____ "purple cow"

In the search box, enter a phrase surrounded by quotation marks. They are required if you want the system to search for a matching phrase.

---

## Boolean:

_____ PURPLE COW

To narrow the focus of your search, enter more terms. The system treats multiple words as part of an AND search.

_____ +cow +dog +cat

A special + (plus) sign can be placed in front of words to require their presence for a page to retrieved. Our search had nine hits with this search strategy.

_____ URL:cats OR URL:dogs-kittens

Though all previous examples of searches can be entered into the simple search box, the use of OR requires taking the Advanced Search link and entering the search strategy in the place for Boolean expressions. In my searches I found that the special commands for searching different parts of Web pages retrieved items I requested along with others I did not request.

Create some sample searches of your own and record your number of hits.

**Number of Hits**          **Search Strategy**

_____          _____

_____          _____

_____          _____

## Family Sites: Family.com

**http://family.disney.com/**

Another approach is to provide Web-based search tools for a given Internet site. Many organizations and institutions provide information and entertainment in this fashion. The organization can carefully and easily set the overall quality of its own site, in the same way that a magazine editor controls the content of every page of paper. The Family.com site by the Disney Company takes this approach. You search only data on the company's hard drives, not sites across the Internet. The Disney search engine is available from its home page. However, all of Disney's Web pages (computer files) are either created by its employees or purchased from others. The amount and growth rate of information in such systems are only a fraction of the size and growth rate of the Internet as a whole.

When you are at the search page for any search system, find the Help or Tips page to learn the special features of the information database. As with any good search system, Family.com has such a page.

# Searching Family.com

## http://family.disney.com/

When multiple search terms are used at the Disney site, AND is assumed. Phrase searching requires quotation marks. Parentheses will not work. Search can use AND, OR, and AND NOT. The link to the Help file appears only after you have completed the first search. The terms here are words you can use to practice searching this Web site. It does not matter whether your word or words are in upper case or lower case; the results will still be the same. Once you have typed these practice words, try some other words and phrases of your own. Record your number of hits as you try these searches below.

## Single Word:

_____ COW

In the search box (i.e., input field), enter a single word. The system retrieves any computer file in the database that contains that word. Our search found 151 Web pages with that word.

## Phrase:

_____ "Purple Cow"

Enter a phrase in the search box. The system treats these two words as a phrase and searches for the words in this sequence. Our search found seven Web pages with that phrase.

## Boolean:

_____ cow or cat or dog

To increase the number of hits, use the OR term between your search words, which can be in any order. Our search found 1,083 pages using these words.

_____ cow and cat and dog

To reduce the number of hits, use the AND term between the words of the search. Our search found 10 pages using these terms.

_____ cat and dog and not cow

To keep some kinds of information from being included, use the AND NOT command. Family.com requires that you indicate a NOT command by writing AND NOT. Our search found 122 pages using this search strategy.

Try some searches on your own and record your number of hits.

**Number of Hits**          **Search Strategy**

_____     _____

_____     _____

## Adding Filters

### *Magellan*

**http://www.mckinley.com/**

The Magellan search system allows users to search for child-safe sites, but it also allows users to look more widely. Users can search the entire Web, which can retrieve adult-only sites; sites with Magellan's written reviews, which may reference adult-only sites; and Green Light sites, which are screened for their child-safe qualities. All reviewed sites are accompanied by a short summary paragraph. One must specifically click a radio button to search for Green-Light-only sites. A Green Light search does not happen by default, though it is very easy to initiate.

Magellan uses Intelligent Concept Extraction (ICE), which is a kind of thesaurus of related ideas for your search terms. Concept searching means that you might search for the phrase "toy car" and have it also return Web pages with the phrase "plastic model kits" in them. The plus sign (+) means that a Web page must contain the term. The minus sign (-) requires that a term not be present. Quotation marks designate phrases. Parentheses are allowed. Searches can also use AND, OR, and NOT, but they must be capitalized.

Given the competitive nature of Internet search systems, one can expect that more systems will develop special search tools for age-appropriate needs. At this time, though, other search systems that provide a greater depth of review and annotation do not designate sites by child safety or family or school appropriateness. Fortunately, these other systems publish their reviews of only the more worthwhile sites. This appears generally to eliminate from their databases the sites that fall outside of the safety zone for our younger citizens. A simple test for unsupervised child safety is to search the online database in question for "adult" and examine some of the retrieved links.

### *Rating/Review Sites*

Table 11.1 is a sampling of some Internet search systems that rate, organize, and review Web sites without specific consideration of age or maturity. Each has its own approach to the use of Boolean logic. Look for Help or Tips pages for assistance.

| Company | Web Address (URL) |
|---|---|
| Argus Clearinghouse | http://www.clearinghouse.net |
| W3C Virtual Library | http://www.w3.org/pub/DataSources/bySubject/Overview.html |
| Lycos—Top 5% | http://point.lycos.com/categories/ |
| McKinley's Magellan | http://www.mckinley.com |
| WebCrawler Select | http://www.webcrawler.com/ |
| NetGuide Live | http://www.netguide.com |
| Excite Reviews | http://www.excite.com/Reviews |
| Yahoo Internet Life | http://www.zdnet.com/yil |
| Internic Directory of Directories | http://www.internic.net/ds/dsdirofdirs.html |
| The Mining Company | http://www.miningco.com/ |
| Channels' Top Sites | http://www.channelsinternet.com/ |

**Table 11.1**

# The Third Level of the Web: Subject Catalogs or Directories

The third level of the Thing category addresses online catalogs. A Yellow Pages section in the telephone book is a kind of catalog. Businesses and institutions pay to have their names and contact information listed under various subject headings. The online catalogs of the third Internet level usually do not charge searchers to look at their listings, and they organize the listed Web sites by various categories and subcategories. The catalogers in this layer do not review Web sites except to determine the topic under which each site should be placed. Nevertheless, this organization by categories is an invaluable resource. From a home page, one can pick a major heading and then follow the subheadings to the Web page resources that are needed. Once you have found the right subject heading, you may find a collection of Web pages and sites on that topic.

Yahoo! remains the premier cataloger of the Internet. Its system is unique among the other cataloging sites. One can not only browse its major headings and subheadings, but can also fully search its catalog. When you search, the system takes you to links for specific Web documents, and also shows which headings and subheadings are being used to place a particular Web page. If a category can be found, a whole set of Web sites with similar information can also be found. However, Yahoo's staff does not evaluate or review these Web pages and sites.

Because it uses the cataloging model of information management, Yahoo!'s database will always contain far fewer links than the entire Internet. To make up for that weakness, upon request Yahoo! can pass your search terms on to other search systems that use software robots that seek to index the entire Internet. (Though a complete index of the Internet is seemingly impossible, because of rapid and continuous additions and deletions to the world's online data, software robots index a significant portion of it.)

## Lycos

### http://www.lycos.com

Lycos provides a wide range of Boolean features for searching. These include AND, OR, NOT, parentheses, and quotation marks for phrases. Pull-down menus and data entry fields are available to make it simpler to use these concepts. Also, Lycos provides commands that address the distance between words in the text: ADJ (meaning adjacent), NEAR, FAR, and BEFORE. Their Pro Search Web page (http://www.lycos.com/help/boolean_help.html) gives examples for their different Boolean features. This distance is an indication of their relationship and importance to each other.

Lycos also makes available child-filtering services for younger searchers. This feature is called Search Guard (Search and Filter Enhanced Technology for Your Net). After you have registered free of charge with Lycos, Search Guard can be turned on and off from a link on the home page and each page of search results. The password that the user provides controls access for activating or deactivating the filtering. Certain words are blocked from being used in searches and offensive sites found by common words are also pushed to the bottom of any list of hits. Though their descriptions of Search Guard indicate that the system filters out adult-oriented sites, it does not discuss other issues including Web pages by hate groups or pages describing and promoting criminal behavior.

## Yahooligans

### http://www.yahooligans.com

Yahooligans is a Web site exclusively for kids and families. All material has been filtered for age appropriateness. Web searching is provided in addition to many categories of activities. When multiple terms are used in a search, an AND relationship is assumed between them. No other possibilities including Boolean terms are provided.

# *Searching with Yahoo!*

## http://www.yahoo.com

Yahoo! provides three degrees of searching capacity. At the easiest level, simply type a single word, or multiple words, in the search box and tap the return or enter key. Using its "intelligent default" search rules, Yahoo! will do a "best possible" hunt through the database. For example, if you enter three words, the system will try to find all three of the terms (an AND search) and put hits containing all three first on the list. If it does not find any within the Yahoo! catalog, it passes the search data on to another search system that returns its results.

The second level of difficulty provides a set of buttons to click. Clicking the Options term to the right of the search box allows the user to pick one of several choices or commands. These include an exact phrase match, matches on all words (AND), and matches on any word (OR).

The highest degree of power comes from using Yahoo!'s Advanced Search Syntax. In this syntax, adding a plus sign (+) to a word forces the word to be found in all the search results. Adding a minus sign or hyphen (-) eliminates any hit containing that word. Other syntax features include: restricting the search to document titles (T:); restricting the search to document URLs (U:); phrase matching (""); wildcard matching (*); and combining syntax if in this order ( +, -, t:, u:, "", and *).

The terms here are words you can use to practice searching this Web site. It does not matter whether your word or words are in uppercase or lowercase; the results will be the same. Once you have typed these practice words, try some other words and phrases of your own. Record your results in the space provided.

## Single Word:

_____ COW

In the search box (i.e., input field), enter a single word. The system retrieves any category in the Yahoo! database that contains that word. Our search found eight categories and 357 sites for COW.

## Set of Words:

_____ cow cat dog

Enter these terms in the search box. Yahoo! treats them as an AND search in which all three terms must be present. If it cannot find them, it passes the data on for a "best search," in which matches with all three items are presented first, then sites matching any two items, and then all pages with any one item—essentially, a prioritized OR search. Our search found no Yahoo! categories or Web sites that matched all three (an AND search).

## Phrase:

_____ "Purple Cow"

Enter a phrase surrounded by quotation marks in the search box. The system treats these two words as a phrase and searches for the words in this sequence. Our search found zero categories and six sites for "Purple Cow."

## Boolean:

_____ cow cat dog

To increase the number of hits, use the Options feature and select the OR choice. The terms can be in any order. Our search found 209 categories and 5,107 sites using these words.

_____ cow cat dog

To reduce the number of hits, use the Options feature and select the AND command. Our search found no documents with these three terms in the Yahoo catalog, and 203 web pages.

_____ +cow -cat -dog

The syntax of this search says to find categories that have the term *cow* but do not contain the terms *cat* or *dog*. Our search found eight categories and 351 sites for +cow -cat -dog. Here are three categories from this set:

Regional: Countries: United Kingdom: Health: Diseases and Conditions: Bovine Spongiform Encephalopathy (BSE)
Science: Biology: Zoology: Animals, Insects, and Pets: Mammals: Cows
Arts: Visual Arts: Computer Generated: ASCII Art: Cows

Create some search strategies of your own and record your results below.

**Number of Hits**          **Search Strategy**

_____          _____

_____          _____

_____          _____

## Subject Search Sites

Table 11.2 is a sampling of some of the Internet search systems that catalog by subject headings. Each has its own approach to the use of Boolean logic. Look for Help, Options, or Tips pages for assistance.

| Company | Web Address (URL) |
|---|---|
| Yahoo! | http://www.yahoo.com |
| Internet Public Library | http://ipl.si.umich.edu/ |
| Virtual Tourist World Map | http://www.vtourist.com/webmap/ |
| Yahoo for Kids! | http://www.yahooligans.com/ |
| Galaxy | http://www.einet.net/ |
| Yanoff's Internet Services List | http://www.spectracom.com/islist/ |
| Librarians' Index | http://sunsite.berkeley.edu/InternetIndex/ |
| LookSmart | http://mulwala.looksmart.com/ |
| CyberDewey | http://ivory.lm.com/~mundie/DDHC/DDH.html |
| Universal Decimal Classification | http://www.bubl.bath.ac.uk/BUBL/Tree.html |
| The Study Web | http://www.studyweb.com/ |

**Table 11.2**

# The Base: Robots

When people are first introduced to Internet searches, it is the robot sites, such as Lycos, Hot-Bot, and Excite, that often provide their initial experiences. Robot systems address the Web territory beyond sites that review and sites that catalog. Neither of these latter two methods for indexing Internet Web sites is capable of providing a comprehensive table of contents of the Internet. This is not just because the number of files on the Internet is so large, but because the Internet's growth and change rates are so high. The only approach that has a chance of staying close to current with this growth of knowledge is a computer-automated search-and-indexing system.

The software programs that manage this indexing feat are referred to as crawlers, bots (robots), wanderers, and spiders. Because of their automated nature, robot-collected search systems raise the previously discussed concerns about child and family safety. Nevertheless, forewarned is forearmed. Users of robot sites can carefully read the short sets of text that accompany the links returned by these search systems. Between the link title and the terse description, one can eliminate the vast majority of inappropriate sites and pages. This procedure is not foolproof, but proper supervision is generally sufficient to quickly close inappropriate pages and move the research effort onward. Users can also add filtering software to screen Web sites. This software will run on your personal computer and prevent access to inappropriate Web sites. However, it may also screen out many useful sites. Users will need to experiment to see how well screening software meets their needs.

Among these automated indexing systems, there are two major designs important to hunters: concept and keyword. In the first design type, the searcher's terms are converted into other concepts that have similar meanings, and those additional concepts are used to retrieve relevant material. In a keyword design, the searcher's words are used just as they are, with little or no further embellishment and extension. Boolean features are often extensive in both types of systems.

# *Searching with Excite*

### http://www.excite.com

Excite's system provides four degrees or levels of searching power. With increasing power comes greater complexity. At each level of searching power, several types of *relevance searching* are available.

All searches are sorted by document relevance. A more relevant document is usually one in which the search term (or terms) appears more often than in another document. With a relevance search, a number indicating the percent of relevance appears next to each of the returned Web page links. The item with the highest percent of relevance appears at the top of a list that provides items in descending order of relevance.

Excite takes the idea of relevance one step further by doing *concept searching*. To search for related or relevant concepts, the search term is compared against a thesaurus of related words. These are often terms you might not have thought of but that could broaden or narrow your search. The top 10 most relevant concepts are then listed below the search box as check boxes. Checking these additional terms can further refine your next search. It is also useful to copy the most relevant of these concepts from the set identified by Excite. You can use these terms later in other search systems that do not provide concept searching. Concept searching is canceled automatically if the Boolean operators AND, OR, AND NOT, and parentheses are used. These operators must appear in all capital letters. Quotation marks can be used around phrases. There is also a way to do concept searching and still use some features of Boolean logic.

Excite also provides another type of relevance search. Next to each Web page link in the search results is the phrase "Click here to perform a search for documents like this one." Excite then uses a formula to extract important terms from the complete Web page and uses them to create a search strategy to look for additional related or relevant Web pages.

The terms here are words you can use to practice searching this Web site. It does not matter whether your word or words are in uppercase or lowercase; the results will be the same. Once you have typed these practice words, try some other words and phrases of your own. Enter your results in the spaces below.

## Single Word:

_____ COW

In the search box (i.e., input field), enter a single word. The system retrieves a set of ten Web pages. Clicking on "[About Your Results]" revealed that there were 62,948 matches for the search on **cow**.

## Phrase:

_____ Purple Cow

Enter a phrase in the search box. Clicking on "[About Your Results]" revealed that our search returned 154,345 matches for the search on **purple cow**.

From *Decision Points: Boolean Logic for Computer Users and Beginning Online Searchers.*
© 1999 Libraries Unlimited, Inc. (800) 237-6124

"Purple Cow"

Do the search again with quotation marks around the phrase. Our search returned 218 matches for **"Purple Cow."** The use of quotation marks is critical to focus your search on the phrase. Without the quotation marks, the search becomes the prioritized OR search described earlier.

## Boolean with Concept Searching:

You can use a form of Boolean logic that does not cancel concept searching. Use the plus sign (+) directly in front of a word. This allows a form of AND searching. This word or words must then appear in any document retrieved. Use a minus sign (-) to exclude any document containing that term. This includes NOT features in a search.

## Power Search—Easy Entry Boolean Form Page
## Without Concept Searching:

Any use of Boolean words turns off concept searching, retrieving just the specified search terms. This form of Boolean can be done from an easy-to-complete form page or by Boolean commands entered directly into the search box.

From the opening Excite search page, look to the right of the text entry box for the link labeled Power Search. Click on it to use the next level of power in searching the Excite system. Power Search is also a link at the bottom of any search result.

_____ cow cat dog

In the Power Search form page, enter these terms in the entry box after the phrase "results CAN contain." This creates an OR search. Our search returned 536,071 matches.

_____ cow cat dog

In the Power Search form page, enter these terms in the entry box after the phrase "results MUST contain." This creates an AND search. This search returned 4,021 matches.

_____ cow

In the Power Search form page, enter this term in the entry box after the phrase "results MUST contain." After the phrase "results MUST NOT contain," enter the words **cat dog**. To increase the number of hits, use the OR term between your search words, which can be in any order. Excite returned 46,475 matches for this query.

## One-Line Boolean Commands Without Concept Searching:

dog AND (cat OR cow) AND NOT lions

Enter these commands in the text entry search box. Boolean terms must be in uppercase. Design and test your own searches in the spaces below.

**Number of Hits**          **Search Strategy**

_____          _____

_____          _____

_____          _____

# Northern Lights

Like Excite, Northern Lights goes beyond the search terms to find related concepts. A search creates two distinct types of results on the same screen. On the right-hand side of the screen is a prioritized list of Web pages based on relevancy. On the left side of the screen, Northern Lights groups the outcome of your search into Custom Search Folders. These folders represent different conceptual subheadings for the topic. If you do not see what you want on the right-hand side, select the most likely choice among the folders on the left. When a folder is opened, Northern Lights immediately creates a new set of folder topics for the next level down. With each new folder level opened, users further narrow the results. Each opening of a folder in the next level downward can remove tens of thousands of pages from consideration, until the best group of items is found. Generally just a few clicks on folders are all that is necessary to reach a small, focused set of Web pages. These folders are not created ahead of time; they are generated dynamically at the time of each search. The folders can be based on subject topics, information type, source, and language.

Like many search engines, the more synonyms and related concepts you enter for the search topic, the more precise your search will be. When in doubt, enter more terms. Boolean concepts can also be used to increase precision. Northern Lights offers full Boolean expressions. Parentheses are allowed and there is no limit to the level of nesting which you can use in a search. It provides for AND, OR, and NOT searches:

Use OR to retrieve documents that include *any* of the search words.

Use NOT to indicate a word that must *not* appear in the documents.

Use quote marks around specific phrases to focus your search on occurrences of the actual phrase.

To take further control of your search, use a + (plus) to indicate words that *must* be present in the documents and a - (minus) for those that must not be present. Two forms of truncation are supported. The * (asterisk) can be used to replace multiple characters. For example, *learn** will find learner, learning, and learned. The % (percent) symbol is used to replace only one symbol. For example, gene%logy will find geneology and genealogy. This system also enables searching within special indices or fields, a feature called "fielded searching." These fields include: URL:, TITLE:, and COMPANY:.

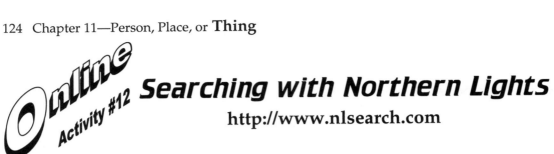

## Searching with Northern Lights

http://www.nlsearch.com

The terms here are words you can use to practice searching this Web site. It does not matter whether the word or words are uppercase or lowercase; the results will be the same. Once you have typed these practice words, try some other words and phrases of your own. Record your own results in the spaces provided.

## Single Word:

_____ COW

In the search box (i.e., input field), enter a single word. The system retrieves a set of 25 Web pages. This search returned 227,211 items, which Northern Lights organized into the following Custom Search Folders: Commercial sites; Educational sites; Dairy cattle farming; Pregnancy; Beef cattle; Epidemics; onWeb.com; Vitamins; Veterinary science; Grain crops; www.ces.uga.edu; all others.

## Phrase:

_____ "Purple Cow"

Enter these words, with the quotation marks, in the search box. This search returned 670 items. For more exact matches and more precise searches, put quotation marks around a phrase.

## Boolean:

_____ Purple Cow

Enter these words in the search box. The system treats these two words as two separate terms, not as a phrase. This search returned 9,236 items. It does a prioritized OR search in which pages containing both instances of the words appear first, followed by those matching only a single term.

_____ cow or cat or dog

This search returned 1,737,707 items. To increase the number of items found, use the OR term between the search words, which can be in any order.

From *Decision Points: Boolean Logic for Computer Users and Beginning Online Searchers.*
© 1999 Libraries Unlimited, Inc. (800) 237-6124

_____ +cat +dog

This search returned 175,866 items. Northern Lights does not use the Boolean term AND. Instead, it uses a plus sign (+). This search pattern does a prioritized OR search in which the first pages, at the top of the list, contain all three terms (if any such items exist); then any combination of two; then pages containing only one of the search terms.

+cat +dog -cow

+cat +dog NOT cow

(cat or kittens) and (dog or puppies) not (Siamese or beagle)

This search returned 157,617 items. To keep certain kinds of information from being included, use the minus sign (-) or the NOT command. The search will return the same results whether you use the minus sign or the NOT command.

Create some searches of your own and record the results below.

**Number of Hits**          **Search Strategy**

_____               _____

_____               _____

_____               _____

From *Decision Points: Boolean Logic for Computer Users and Beginning Online Searchers.*
© 1999 Libraries Unlimited, Inc. (800) 237-6124

# *Searching with HotBot*

### http://www.hotbot.com/

HotBot does a complete index of every word it finds on a Web page. It currently claims to have indexed more than 110 million Web pages. Searches use this full index of words. Hot-Bot counters the problem of information glut with a lengthy set of search options. The more options, the more precise a search can be. The more precise the search, the fewer items retrieved—but the greater the chance that those items will be precisely what is needed. In all types of searching, the next search can look through the results of the search just completed (Revise Search) or can be a new search, once again looking through the entire HotBot database (New Search).

From HotBot's opening screen under the search box, a pull-down menu provides seven basic choices: all the terms, any of the terms, the exact phrase, words in the title, the person, links to this URL, or the Boolean phrase. These search settings can be further refined: by a range of dates selected from a pull-down menu; by language; and by media type, including image, audio, video, and Java Script.

A second level of search capacity is available through the "More Search Options" button. This option includes all the previous options but also provides a form page with data entry fields for additional search terms, with pull-down commands for further Boolean control and range of words, selection by language and continent, manual entry for a date of your choice, more media types, and a depth search option.

A third level is provided by full Boolean terminology: AND, &; OR, |; NOT, !; and parentheses ( ); plus quotation marks ("") to define a phrase. HotBot also provides a long list of "meta words" which are shortcuts to non-text searches. For example, "title:animals" searches only the page title. Explore the Help page of a long list of meta words. Wildcard searches use * (asterisk). Searches are case-sensitive only if any letter in the search strategy is capitalized. To use any Boolean terms, the user must first select "Boolean phrase" from the "all the words" menu.

The terms here are words you can use to practice searching this Web site. It does not matter whether the word or words are in uppercase or lowercase; the results will be the same. Once you have typed these practice words, try some other words and phrases of your own. Enter the number of hits you find in the spaces below.

## Single Word:

_____ COWS

Enter a single word in the search box. The system retrieves any computer file in the database that contains that word. Our search found 282,938 Web pages with that word.

## Phrase:

_____ Purple Cow

Enter these words in the search box. This time select the exact match from the pull-down menu. This search returned 1,290 matches.

## Boolean: (Remember to select "Boolean phrase.")

_____ Purple Cow

Enter these words in the search box. The system defaults to searching for all the words (an AND search) unless a different choice is selected from the pull-down menu. The system treats two words as two separate terms, not as a phrase, when the choice "all the words" is selected. This search returned 17,289 matches.

_____ cow cat dog

Select the choice "any of the words" from the pull-down menu. This is a type of Boolean OR search. This search found 2,349,891 matches.

_____ +cat +dog -cow

Select the choice "all the words" from the pull-down menu. This search returned 182,689 matches. To keep certain kinds of information from being included, use the minus sign (-), which acts as the Boolean term NOT.

## Examples of Boolean Logic's Power to Narrow Your Search:

**Games:**

game or games or play or toy or toys

8,338,020 matches

(boy or girl) and (game or games or play or toy or toys)

728,670 matches

"board games" and (boy or girl) and (game or games or play or toy or toys)

2,210 matches

Thanksgiving and "board games" and (boy or girl) and (game or games or play or toy or toys) not (Halloween or Christmas)

25 matches

**Fish:**

fish or fishing

11,426,650 matches

(fish or fishing) and (worm or worms or bait)

64,190 matches (95 percent reduction of data from previous search)

(fish or fishing) and (worm or worms or bait) and (poles or rod) and (pond or lake or stream) NOT (money or job or work) and (story or tale)

710 matches (99 percent reduction from previous search)

freshwater (fish or fishing) and (worm or worms or bait) and (poles or rod) and (pond or lake or stream) NOT (money or job or work) and (story or tale)

66 matches (91 percent reduction from previous search)

free and (bluegill and catfish) and (story or tale) and (fish or fishing) and (worm or worms or bait) and (poles or rod) and (pond or lake or stream) NOT (money or job or work)

5 matches (92 percent reduction from previous search)

Create some searches of your own. Enter the results and strategies below.

**Number of Hits**                **Search Strategy**

_____              _____

_____              _____

_____              _____

## Automated Search Routines

Table 11.3 is a sampling of some of the Internet search systems that use automated software routines (bots or spiders) to find and index Web sites and Web pages. Each has its own approach to the use of Boolean logic. Look for the Help or Tips pages for assistance at these sites.

| Company | Web Address (URL) |
|---|---|
| Excite | http://www.excite.com/ |
| Northern Lights | http://www.nlsearch.com/ |
| Alta Vista | http://www.altavista.digital.com/ |
| OpenText | http://www.opentext.com |
| InfoSeek | http://www.infoseek.com |
| HotBot | http://www.hotbot.com/index.html |
| Lycos | http://www.lycos.com |
| Webcrawler | http://www.webcrawler.com |
| MetaCrawler | http://www.metacrawler.com |
| Meta-SavvySearch | http://savvy.cs.colostate.edu:2000/ |
| Meta-search.com | http://www.search.com/ |
| Internet Sleuth | http://www.isleuth.com/ |
| Personal Newsfeeds | http://www.yahoo.com/News_and_Media/Personalized_News/ |
| Intelligent Agents | http://www.yahoo.com/Business_and_Economy/Companies/Computers/Software/Internet/Intelligent_Agents/ |

**Table 11.3**

## Final Decision Points

Through the many options for finding information that have been discussed so far, you can quickly gather a mountain of facts, figures, and ideas. Assuming that the information passes all the decision points discussed so far, such as safety, relevance, and accuracy, you face still another decision not present in the physical world. How can you store or keep this information?

If you receive a book, you store it by putting it on the shelf. The book is its own storage system. This is not true in the electronic world. There must be electronic containers for everything that is to be kept. Our species has an amazing variety of terms for containers: boxes, crates, gunnysacks, backpacks, jars, baskets, drawers, folders, and more. Electronic hunters might use their favorite term for *container* to make the hunt more fun. Will the Thing caught be stored in a "gunnysack" that is a diskette, a fixed hard drive, a removable hard drive such as a ZIP disk, or a compact disc—or should it be sent to the printer? Also, once information has been reviewed, there may be no need to keep it. Internet hunters may simply delete what they have found after a quick read.

There are common procedures for keeping and managing what you have found in the virtual world. In all cases they involve giving the information further organization by placing the data into appropriately named folders. Printing information and placing it into paper folders is a common, well-understood operation. Perhaps not so well utilized are electronic folders. Every operating system has a procedure for creating electronic folders or directories under which information can be further grouped and organized. This process should be used when electronic hunters return to their desktops with new information. If an entire Web page or Internet file is to be saved, these project pieces should be put in appropriately labeled electronic folders. Folders can be further organized inside other electronic folders for several levels (a process that does not work well with paper folders).

Often you will want to save only a fraction of a Web page. With Web page text, simply click and drag across the text of interest. Once the text is selected use the Copy command under Edit in the menu bar. Next, open a window to a word-processing screen, position the cursor at the appropriate place on the page, and give the Paste command. The data once on an Internet Web page should appear in the word processor window. Text, numbers, images, sounds, and video can be moved from Internet screens to other applications such as word processors, databases, and spreadsheets. Further, many common word processors (e.g., Clarisworks, WordPerfect, and Microsoft Word) include electronic outlining features. As information is retrieved, it can be placed under various outline headings. Your data organization can build within the word processing window as you find information.

## Serving Ideas

Hunting in cyberspace takes time, but it should not be hurried. If the hunting is not rushed, the process stimulates creative and critical ideas in the hunters themselves. It is important that these personal ideas be stored as well. The need to store both personal ideas and the ideas of others means that hunters must carefully label the information according to its ownership or source. The practice of citing information has a long tradition in paper technology. The only real addition to the citation form of an Internet source is the address of the Web page, its uniform resource locator (URL). Once stored, these personal ideas play a critical role in fitting the information that has been found to the situation that stirred the hunter to action in the first place.

Eventually a composition emerges. Its evaluation benefits greatly from the insight of those who did not create it. Writers and composers need to allow time for their own reflection and the reflection of other thinkers. As was discussed earlier, one of the great weaknesses of the bottom layer of the pyramid—the virtual or Internet system—is that the works created from the captures of the hunt are too often taken undercooked to the Internet table. The ease with which electronic data can go from the hunter's net to cooking pot (word processor) to serving dish (an Internet Web server) is the reason for the poor quality of much that is found there. In the Information Age, it can take only seconds, often at no expense to those who cooked up the ideas, for data to move from local brain to global brain. More so than with the taste of stew on a stove, many cooks are needed to keep the quality of information at the highest levels. When information is passed to publishers using older, more expensive technologies such as paper, a series of editors filters and reforms the information. The challenge to the education system of the new century is to develop new systems of editing for the Internet. These systems should be of such caliber that our young writers and composers will eagerly flock to them to improve and enhance themselves and their creations.

Once a mix of information has been organized and responsibly edited, it will undoubtedly evoke a response. This response, among those who were the primary audience for the fare of the hunter turned composer/cook, is significant. Whatever improvements develop in our communities do so through this interaction between new ideas and the responses to them—this is what makes personal and civic growth possible. After information is shared with those who need it immediately, it can be returned to the larger forest of information. Those who share should consider how their ideas will work their way back up through the layers of the information pyramid.

Internet information servers can increasingly be found in businesses and public and private institutions. Information organizers and composers need merely to contact their administrator to ask for the procedure and permission to place their work where it will be visible to others on the global network. For those whose desktops have a direct connection to the Internet, Web server software options are inexpensive or free, and are more and more frequently an option within the owner's operating systems and applications. Every desktop computer can easily reserve a special part of its hard drive for use as an Internet information server, the resources of which are made known to the information search systems previously discussed. As hunters move on to other activities and sleep, information robots find and note the presence of new elements in the forest by adding them to the search engines.

Knowledge workers should also seek entry to the middle and top layers of the information pyramid. Publishers of books, journals, magazines, and other media have added power to advertise these works to a large audience that might not otherwise locate a work in the cacophony of the Internet. When ideas become a part of the thinking of recognized experts in a field of interest, those who began their work as hunters in the forest know that their achievements have reached the top of the pyramid.

A vast and growing set of tools now exists to construct the information world of the twenty-first century. Guiding us through many decision points, these tools and Boolean logic have become part of a cycle of finding, managing, and growing knowledge. In this manner, the work of a few is positioned to nourish the next set of hunters who step into the information realm.

# Answer Key

⟹

## Answer Key—Activity #1

1. If I hike five more miles, then I will earn my 50-Mile pin for Scouts.

2. If I give two more pints of blood, then I will earn a one-gallon pin from the Red Cross.

3. If I drop .08 seconds off my 100-meter swim time, then I can participate in the competition.

4. If I improve my sight-reading score by 20%, then I will take First Chair in the band.

5. If I raise my batting average by .05, then I will qualify for the All-Stars.

6. If I improve my grade point average by .5, then I will make the honor roll.

7. If I read four more 200-page books, then I will attend the Accelerated Readers party.

8. If I can cut 250 words from my essay, then I can submit it to the essay contest.

## Sample Responses: Activity #2
### (Individual responses may vary.)

1. If I remember my bathing suit, then I will swim today.

2. If I win the trombone competition, then I will play First Chair.

3. If I can get to the store to buy more toothpicks, then I will finish my bridge.

4. If I can locate an address for *Sports* magazine, then I will renew my subscription.

5. If there is open time in the computer lab today, then I will play on the computer.

6. If there is an available court, I will play racquetball after school.

7. If I complete five hours of orientation, then I can become a library aide.

8. If I can get someone to take me home afterwards, then I can play in the recorder ensemble after school.

# Sample Answers—Activity #3
## (Individual responses may vary.)

**Section 1:**
1. I would like to walk a section of the Appalachian Trail.
2. I would like to learn to do kayak rolls.

**Section 2:**
1. I would like to walk a section of the Appalachian Trail but I don't have anyone to go with.
2. I would like to learn to do kayak rolls but I need a good teacher to show me how.

**Section 3:**
1. If I locate and join a hiking club, then I may meet a walking partner so I can walk a section of the Appalachian Trail.
2. If I call around and locate a kayak instruction class, then I will learn to do a kayak roll.

# Answer Key—Activity #4

**Possible responses:**
1. **Condition affirmative:** If I backpack five more miles I can earn my 50-Mile pin from Scouts.
   **Condition negative:** If I do not backpack five more miles, then I will not earn my 50-Mile pin.
2. **Affirmative:** If I read 12 more books, then I can become a member of the One Hundred Book Club.
   **Negative:** If I do not read 12 more books, then I cannot become a member of the One Hundred Book Club.
3. **Affirmative:** If I donate two more pints of blood, then I will earn my Red Cross one-gallon pin.
   **Negative:** If I do not donate two more pints of blood, then I will not earn my Red Cross one-gallon pin.
4. **Affirmative:** If I drop three seconds off my 25-yard backstroke time, then I will qualify for the fastest heat.
   **Negative:** If I do not drop three seconds off my 25-yard backstroke time, then I will not qualify for the fastest heat.
5. **Affirmative:** If I submit my Web page design by August 15, then I will be included in the online contest.
   **Negative:** If I do not submit my Web page design by August 15, then I will not be included in the online contest.

# Answer Key—Activity #5

**Possible responses:**

1.   If you do not close the door, then the blinking light will stay on.

2.   If you do not close the window, then the alarm will continue to sound.

3.   If a key is not used, then an alarm will sound.

4.   If the correct security code is not typed in, then the local police will be automatically notified.

5.   If the bank card access number is not entered correctly, then the ATM will take the card.

6.   If you close and lock all the doors, then the alarm will not sound.

7.   If you close all the windows and lock them, then the flood light will not come on.

8.   If you use the key properly, then the alarm will not sound.

9.   If you type the security code in properly, then the police will not be notified.

10.   If the bank card access number is entered correctly, then the ATM will not take the card.

# Answer Key—Activity #6

1.   *f*
2.   *a*
3.   *d*
4.   *c*
5.   *e*
6.   *b*

# Answer Key: Activity #7

1.   Outcome *b*
2.   IF *c*
3.   Negative *d*
4.   Positive *h*
5.   THEN *g*
6.   Condition *f*
7.   Series *e*
8.   Logic *a*

## Sample Answers—Activity #8

IF
1. the fuel tank is full

AND
2. the wind speeds are low

AND
3. the weather is favorable

AND
4. the pressure in the tanks is normal

AND
5. the on-board control panel is functioning properly

AND
6. the near-by grounds crew has evacuated

AND
7. the heat shield has been checked three times

AND
8. all back-up systems have checked out OK

AND
9. the oxygen levels are appropriate in the shuttle

AND
10. the astronauts are secured in place

THEN Blastoff!

## Answer Key—Activity #9

Fill in the chart with + for a closed switch and – for an open switch. Any combination can go in any column. As you begin in the third column, look back to columns one and two and do not duplicate those patterns. Then as you fill in the fourth column, continue to look back so that each new column you make is different from the preceding ones.

## Answer Key—Activity #10

### #1 and #2

"Swimmers" would call up the *most* listings because the word has not been modified to exclude phrases such as "dogs are good swimmers."

Swimmers AND gold medalists would call up *fewer* listings because each term would need to be included in the document. These articles would probably focus on human swimmers since dogs generally don't win gold medals for swimming.

## #3 and #4

"Dogs" would call up the most listings because any time dogs appear in a document if would be cited. For example, you might get a fiction story that said, "Nancy had loved dogs her whole life." This, of course, would not necessarily be a good reference book about dogs.

"Dogs AND sleds" would call up the fewest listings because only those books that wrote about sled dogs would be referenced. If that is the topic you were seeking, this search strategy would be very useful.

## #5 and #6

"Boy Scouts" would cite numerous listings about activities and Troops around the world. This would locate a great deal of general information about Boy Scouting.

"Boy scouts AND Eagle Awards" would call up less information because it would be limiting the search to only those articles that mention Eagle awards in association with Boy Scouts.

## #7 and #8

"Playwrights" would call up a large number of playwrights' names, their works, their autobiographies, and so on, both past and present, from around the world.

"American AND playwrights" would locate only document sources that discussed American playwrights. That is not to say that foreign playwrights would not be included.

## #9 and #10

"Musicals" would find articles where that word is used, not necessarily in connection with Broadway. An article might include a statement such as "Musicals are an American heritage," but there might be no mention of Broadway.

"Broadway AND musicals" would find fewer articles (in theory) than would the search term "musicals." However, any given article might include information about musicals other than Broadway musicals. At least you would be assured that the article included your desired topic of "Broadway musicals."

## #11 and #12

"Heisman trophies AND football" would call up more specific articles about football that mention Heisman. Presumably there would be fewer of these articles than articles in general about football.

"Football" would cite numerous articles wherever the word *football* is mentioned.

## #13 and #14

This allows the students to have a chance at selecting a term and then modifying it to use as an AND search. Be sure the two terms are associated in some way to get the most meaningful search terms.

# Sample Answers—Activity #11

**Possible search strategies:**
1. Lincoln AND debates
1. Washington AND Continental Congress
1. Reagan AND Berlin Wall

# Answer Key—Activity #12

**Search #1: electric AND eel**                    **Search #2: "electric eel"**

a.  Aaron's dive shop to see a picture of an electric eel
    Search #2. The search identified the article by matching the exact words.

b.  Australian eel farms are electrically monitored
    Search #1. The search identified an article containing each of the words, but not necessarily in that sequence or being used to reference each other. The word "electric" would be identified in "electrically" in most searches.

c.  Cabins on the Eel river with no electric hook-up
    Search #1. The search identified an article containing each of the words, but not necessarily in that sequence or being used to reference each other.

d.  A British rock group named the "Electric Eels"
    Search #2. Although this is not about the creature, this search identified a phrase by exact word match. This is an example of how even an exact word match may not always give you exactly what you want.

e.  Cooking curried eel on an electric stove
    Search #1. This search gave you an interesting topic, but does not specifically talk about electric eel recipes, just eel recipes.

f.  Electric eels are being used to kill pain
    Search #2. This search did identify an article specifically about electric eels.

g.  "The Eel" (author, Unagi) is an electric story
    Search #1. Once again, both words were found to share the same article, but are not related to the specific topic of electric eels.

h.  Place an order for an eel using an electric order form
    Search #1. Both keywords were found in this article, but no reference to an electric Eel was included.

i.  Generating electric current on the Eel River
    Search #1. Fooled again. No electric eels here.

j.  Electric shock being used to stun unwanted eels that have invaded an unnatural habitat
    Search #1. Both keywords are present, but no electric eels.

k.  Watching the Eels play soccer created an electric atmosphere
    Search #1. It wasn't electric eels playing soccer, only the team, the Eels, playing electrically.

l.  The Eels ball club playing a night game under electric lights
    Search #1. Both search terms are present here, but no electric eels in sight.

# Sample responses—Activity #13

1. movie/Disney/mermaid
2. movie/Independence Day/disaster
3. movie/Apollo 13/spacecraft
4. movie/Speed/bus
5. movie/Tibet/Pitt (Brad)

**Section 2:**

2. Fourth of July, July 4, 1976, American holidays
3. NASA, space program, space shuttle, Mercury, astronauts
4. jets, race cars, trains
5. Himalaya, Tibetan monks, Mt. Everest

# Answer Key—Activity #14

1. "not to be disqualified" is +
2. "not to be awarded the certificate" is –
3. "not to get a traffic ticket" is +
4. "not to have to attend Saturday school to make up the time" is +
5. "not to be counted absent" is +
6. "not to be allowed to attend the pep rally" is –
7. "par score will not increase" is + (In golf, the lower the score is, the better.)
8. "not to have to depend on your friend for a ride" is +
9. "not to be allowed to enter" is –
10. "not to be denied entrance" is +
11. "not be counted tardy" is +
12. "not be fined" is +

# Sample Responses—Activity #15

1. If there is no school AND If the snow doesn't melt
2. If you read each night AND If you do all your written assignments
3. THEN you will go parasailing
4. If the wallet is not empty AND If the refrigerator is not stocked
5. If the bike gets fixed AND If the weather is sunny

# Sample Responses—Activity #16

1.  Tacos

    chicken AND sour cream NOT black olives

2.  Submarine sandwiches

    turkey AND cheese NOT mayonnaise

3.  Hamburgers

    lettuce AND tomatoes NOT pickles

4.  Hot dogs

    chili AND cole slaw NOT onions

5.  Baked potato

    bacon bits AND sour cream AND cheese NOT chives

# Sample Responses—Activity #17

IF

1.  vaccum the living room

    OR

2.  categorize recycling items

    OR

3.  empty kitchen trash

    OR

4.  feed the dogs

    OR

5.  walk the dogs

    OR

6.  fold laundry

    OR

7.  put a load in the wash

    OR

8.  sweep the kitchen floor

    OR

9.  unload the dishwasher

    OR

10. distribute the mail to family members

    The student is encouraged to respond with chores unique to his home.

## Sample Responses—Activity #18

1. If wind speed exceeds safety level

    OR

2. If water level exceeds safety level

    OR

3. If low temperature (ice forming) exceeds safety level

    OR

4. If water flow rate exceeds safety level

    OR

5. If pressure against the containment walls exceeds safety level

    THEN action is taken to alter the containment level.

## Answer Key—Activity #19

1. fewer

    more

2. fewer

    more

3. more

    fewer

4. fewer

    more

5. more

    fewer

6. fewer

    more

7. The student is encouraged to provide examples meaningful to an interest of his/hers.

# Sample Answers—Activity #20

1. ocean OR *d* (sea)
2. horse OR *g* (equestrian)
3. rain OR *h* (precipitation)
4. gale OR *b* (hurricane)
5. rocks OR *a* (stones)
6. earth OR *f* (environment)
7. aquanaut OR *c* (SCUBA)
8. astronomy OR *e* (stars)
9. homes OR *i* (habitats)
10. rocket OR *j* (spaceships)

# Answer Key—Activity #21

1. season*

**Answers to be circled:**

Seasons, seasonal, Season's Greetings

(pre-season, post-season, and unseasonable would not be called up because they do not begin with "s-e-a-s-o-n.")

2. Poison*

**Answers to be circled:**

Poisonous, poisonous gases, poisonous snakes (nonpoisonous would not be called up because it does not begin with "p-o-i-s-o-n.")

3. elect*

**Answers to be circled:**

elected officials, electric circuits, elections, electronics, electrocuted

4. marine*

**Answers to be circled:**

Marine Corps, mariner (submarine would not be called up because it does not begin with "m-a-r-i-n-e.")

5. civil*

**Possible answers:**

civilian, Civil Rights, civil service, civil servants, civil engineering

6. rest*

**Possible answers:**

restrooms, rest homes, restaurant, rest stops

## Sample Answers—Activity #22

1.  Completed for you.

2.  catsup
    OR                 NO(T) onions
    mustard

3.  chicken
    OR                 NO(T) sour cream
    beef

4.  turkey
    OR                 NO(T) jalapeno peppers
    chicken

5.  chocolate
    OR                 NO(T) marshmallow
    strawberry

## Sample Answers—Activity #23

1.  a.  catsup AND mustard NOT pickles

    b.  lettuce AND tomato AND catsup NOT onions

2.  a.  beef AND bean NOT chicken

    b.  beef AND bean AND sour cream NOT green onions

3.  a.  ham AND cheese NOT green peppers

    b.  turkey AND lettuce AND tomato NOT mayonnaise

## Sample Answers—Activity #24

1.  Sample provided in text.

2.  Sample provided in text.

3.  golf OR tennis NOT badminton

4.  pets OR dogs NOT rabbits

5.  ducks OR chickens NOT turkeys

## Sample Responses—Activity #25

1.  maple OR trees NOT "Maple Leafs" (referring to the Toronto ice hockey team)

2.  birds OR hawks NOT Seahawks (referring to the Seattle Seahawks)

3.  birds OR cardinals NOT Cardinals (referring to the St. Louis Cardinals baseball team)

4.  cattle OR bulls NOT Bulls (referring to the Chicago Bulls basketball team)

5.  hornets OR wasps NOT Hornets (referring to the Charlotte Hornets basketball team)

6.  The intended search is to find items about birds, not the rock group named "Counting Crows."

7.  The intended search here is to find items about "Counting Crows," the rock group, and to rule out articles about crows and birds.

8.  The intended search is to identify items about race, race relations, and civil rights, and to rule out any references to "races."

9.  The intended search is to identify items that discuss the use of space as it relates to architecture, not outer space.

10. The intended search is to identify items that discuss chemical properties of acids and bases rather than baseball.

## Sample Responses—Activity #26

thin and crispy AND sausage AND extra cheese

## Answer Key—Activity #27

1.  Bridge #1 AND Bridge #2 AND Ferry #3

    OR

2.  Ferry #1 AND Ferry #2                    Reach destination

    OR

3.  Ferry #1 AND Bridge #2 AND Ferry #3

    OR

4.  Bridge #1 AND Ferry #2

# Table of Selected Boolean Features

# Table of Selected Boolean Features

| Site | Discussed Sites & Numbered Activities | URL (http://) | Family Filtered | AND | OR | NOT | Parentheses | Phrases |
|---|---|---|---|---|---|---|---|---|
| **Person (people, organizations)** | | | | | | | | |
| PeopleFind from Lycos | | www.lycos.com peoplefind/ | (NA) | | | | | |
| People Search from Yahoo | | people.yahoo.com/ | (NA) | | | | | |
| BigBook from GTE | | www.bigbook.com/ | (NA) | (spaces) | (commas) | | | |
| Cyberfiber Newsgroups | | www.cyberfiber.com/ | no | radio button | radio button | | | |
| DejaNews | 1 | www.dejanews.com/ | available | pull-down, and, & | pull-down, or, \| | pull-down, not, &! | yes | "" |
| Liszt | | www.liszt.com/ | no | pull-down, and | pull-down, or | not | yes | "" |
| **Place (Shelves)** | | | | | | | | |
| Cleveland Public Library | 2 | www.cpl.org/ | yes | and | or | not | yes | no |
| Canton Public Library | 3 | metronet.lib.mi.us/CANT/homepage.html | yes | and | or | | yes | (no) |
| Public Library of Nashville and Davidson County | 4 | waldo.nashv.lib.tn.us/ | yes | and | or | | yes | (no) |
| Amazon Bookstore | 5 | www.amazon.com/ | yes | and | or | not | yes | "" |
| Follett | 6 | www.ourlibrary/ | yes | and | or | not | no | (no) |
| Library of Congress | 7 | telnet://locis.loc.gov/ | yes | and | or | not | yes | (no) |

# Thing (Drives)

| Name | # | URL | | AND | OR | NOT | | Phrase |
|---|---|---|---|---|---|---|---|---|
| AltaVista | 8 | www.altavista.com/ | available | and, + | or | not, - | yes | "" |
| Family.com | 9 | family.disney.com/ | yes | and | or | and not | no | "" |
| Magellan | | www.mckinley.com/ | available | AND, + | OR | NOT, - | yes | "" |
| Lycos | | www.lycos.com/ | available | pull-down, and, + | pull-down, or | not, - | yes | "" |
| Yahooligans | 10 | www.yahooligans.com/ | yes | | | | | |
| Yahoo | 10 | www.yahoo.com/ | no | radio buttons, + | radio buttons | - | no | "" |
| Excite | 11 | www.excite.com/ | no | pull-down, AND, + | pull-down, OR | pull-down, AND NOT, - | yes | pull-down, "" |
| Northern Lights | 12 | www.nlsearch.com/ | no | and, + | or | not, - | yes | "" |
| HotBot | 13 | www.hotbot.com/ | no | pull-down, and, & | pull-down, or, \| | pull-down, not, ! | yes | "" |

To keep the table compact, explanations are provided outside the table. If the Boolean terms are in uppercase (e.g., AND, OR), then the system requires that they be entered in uppercase. If the terms are in lowercase, then the system does not care whether lower or uppercase is used. When the phrase "pull-down" is used in the table, it means that there is a screen in which you can click on a pull-down menu in the Web page and select the needed command. The phrase "radio-button" refers to small circles on the Web page that activate a particular feature. The term "(spaces)" means to use the space bar between words to mean the same as AND. The term "(commas)" means to put commas between words to have the OR equivalent.

From *Decision Points: Boolean Logic for Computer Users and Beginning Online Searchers.*
© 1999 Libraries Unlimited, Inc. (800) 237-6124

# Index

| for OR logic, 50, 63
| for pipe searches, 32
" " (quotation marks) for phrase searches, 30
& (ampersand) for AND logic, 30
* (asterisk) for partial-word searches, 55
+ (plus sign) for AND logic, 30
- (minus sign) for NOR (NOT-OR) logic, 63

Acses, 97
Address books, 82
Affirmative. *See* Positive conditions; Positive outcomes
Age-appropriate searching family Internet sites, 114–16, 116tab, 117
  in libraries, physical, 88, 90
  in newsgroups, 84
  in online bookstores, 96, 97
  reviewed Internet sites, 110–11, 116, 116tab
  virtual world, decisions about, 108
Alta Vista, 50, 63, 111–13
Amazon Bookstore, 96–97, 98–99
Ampersand (&) for AND logic, 30
AND logic
  ampersand (&) for, 30
  for circuit, series (simple), 22fig, 22–23, 23fig
  for decision making, combining OR logic, 67–71, 74
  defined, 15fig, 15–16, 16fig
  for everyday experiences, 15–20, 17fig
  for excluding material in searches, 25, 27–28
  in flowcharts, 27–28, 28fig
  focus to find concept, 27–28
  as identifier (operator) for searching databases, 25, 25fig
  If-Then logic and, 18fig, 18–20
  OR logic, comparison, 51
  pipe searches, 32
  plus sign (+) for, 30
  research time, saving with, 27–28
  searching databases with, 25, 27–28, 30, 32, 77
  syntax of search engines and, 30, 32
  truth tables for, 15tab, 16tab, 17tab

AND/AND/OR logic, 68, 68fig
AND/OR/AND logic, 67, 67fig
Argus Clearinghouse, 116tab
Associations, learned, 2
Asterisk (*) for partial-word searches, 55
Automated search routines, 110, 120–29, 129tab
AV Family Filter (Alta Vista), 111

Barnes & Noble, 96, 97
Berkeley (California) Public Library's Web pages, 90
BigBook (GTE) site, 82–83
Blocking software, 110–11, 116, 120
Books and resources for K-12, 90, 96, 97. *See also* Age-appropriate searching
Bookstores, 96–99
Boole, George, 1–2
Boolean algebra, 1–2
Boolean logic, 1–2. *See also* AND logic; Conditions; Decision making; If-Then logic; NAND (NOT-AND) logic; NOR (NOT-OR) logic; NOT logic; OR logic; Outcomes; Searching tips; Truth tables
Boston (Massachusetts) Public Library's Web pages, 90
Bots, 120–29, 129tab

Canton (Michigan) Public Library, 92–93
Case-sensitivity and searching, 63
Catalogs, online, 117–20, 120tab
*Caveat emptor* (searcher beware), 79, 81, 85–86, 108
Channels' Top Sites, 116tab
Children's material. *See* Age-appropriate searching
Choices. *See* OR logic
Circuits
  integrated, 67
  parallel and OR logic, 47fig, 47–48
  series (simple) and AND logic, 22fig, 22–23, 23fig
Cleveland (Ohio) Library, 91
Commercial online publications, 109
Computer networks. *See* Internet

Computers
  chips, 67
  conditions as inputs for, 22–23
  half-life of files, 88
  If-Then logic for, 12
  inputs, defined, 12
  integrated circuits, 67
  personal computers, knowledge on, 76
Concept automated indexing systems, 120
Conditions. *See also* AND logic; If-Then
      logic; NAND (NOT-AND) logic;
      NOR (NOT-OR) logic; NOT logic;
      OR logic; Outcome
  defined, 2, 5
  as inputs for computers, 22–23
  negative, 8, 10
  number of, effect on outcome, 18, 45
  positive, 8, 10, 15–20
  as prerequisites for outcome, 5
  sequence (order) of, 12
Crawlers, 120–28
CyberDewey, 120tab
CyberFiber site, 83

Data Research Associates (DRA), 91
Data structures, 78
Database syntax (rules), 30, 32, 50, 63–64.
    *See also* Searching tips
Decision making. *See also* Boolean logic;
    Knowledge in information age; Per-
    son information system; Place infor-
    mation system; Searching tips; Thing
    information system
  decision points for, 1–2
  integrated, 67–71, 74
  learning (previous) and, 74
DejaNews site, 84, 85
Disney Company family site, 114–15
DRA (Data Research Associates), 91

Electronic data storage, 107–8
Email addresses sources, 82
Email conferences, 83
Encyclopaedia Britannica online resource,
    109
Excite, 121–22
Excite Reviews, 116tab
Excluding material in searches, 25, 27–28,
    40, 63
Expanding searches, 51, 55

Family sites, 111–15. *See also* Age-
    appropriate searching
Family.com (Disney site), 114–15
File-content searching, 77
Filtering software, 110–11, 116, 120
"Find" command, 76–77
First Amendment rights, 110
Flowcharts and AND logic, 27–28, 28fig
Focus to find concept, 27–28
Folders, electronic, 130
Follett Incorporated, 100–2
Freedom of expression, 110
Full-text publications, 109

Galaxy, 120tab

Half-life of computer files, 88
HotBot, 126–28, 129tab
Hunting. *See* Searching tips

ICE (Intelligent Concept Extraction), 116
Ideas, personal, 130–31
If-Then logic
  AND logic and, 18fig, 18–20
  for computers, 12
  statements, 8
III (Innovative Interfaces, Inc.), 92–94
Indexing systems, automated, 120
Information systems. *See* Person informa-
    tion system; Place information sys-
    tem; Searching tips; Thing
    information system
Informed decisions, 1
InfoSeek, 50, 129tab
Innovative Interfaces, Inc. (III), 92–94
Inputs, for computers, 12, 22–23
Intelligent Agents, 129tab
Intelligent Concept Extraction (ICE), 116
Internet. *See also* Searching tips; World
    Wide Web
  defined, 77
  problems with, 107–9
  reviewed (professionally) sites, 110–11,
    116, 116tab
Internet Life (Yahoo!), 116tab
Internet Public Library, 120tab
Internet Sleuth, 129tab
Internic Directory of Directories, 116tab
Intranets, 77
Inversions (opposite outcomes), 10

Juvenile material. *See* Age-appropriate searching

Keyword automated indexing systems, 120
Keyword (root word) searches, 55
Knowledge in information age, 75–80. *See also* Age-appropriate searching; Person information system; Place information system; Searching tips; Thing information system

Languages, programming, 1
LC (Library of Congress) site, 89, 103
Librarians' Index, 120tab
Libraries
 city, 90
 online, 89–95
 school, 100–2
 versus Web pages, 88–89
Library of Congress Information System (LOCIS), 89, 103–6
Library of Congress (LC) site, 89, 103
Listservs (mailing lists), 83, 85–86
Liszt, 85
Local area network computers, 77
LOCIS (Library of Congress Information System), 89, 103–6
Logic. *See* Boolean logic
LookSmart, 120tab
Lycos
 People Find Service, 81–82
 Phone Number database, 82
 Search Guard, 117
 searching with, 50, 117, 129tab
 Top 5% search system, 116tab
 White Pages, 81–82

Magellan, 116
Mailing lists (listservs), 83, 85–86
Managing information, 129–31
Meta-SavvySearch, 129tab
Meta-search.com, 129tab
Mining Company, The, 116tab
Minus sign (-) for NOR (NOT-OR) logic, 63

NAND (NOT-AND) logic
 defined, 35fig, 35–36, 38, 40fig
 double negatives, 36
 searching databases with, 40, 40fig
 truth tables for, 36tab
Narrowing searches, 25, 27–28, 32, 40, 51, 59

Negative conditions, 8, 10
Negative outcome, 10
NetGuide Live, 116tab
Newsfeed to newsgroups, 83
Newsgroups, 83–85
NOR (NOT-OR) logic
 defined, 57fig, 57–58
 minus sign (-) for, 63
 pipe (|) for, 63
 searching databases with, 58–59
 syntax of search engines and, 63–64
 truth table for, 58tab
Northern Lights, 123–25
NOT logic, 10. *See also* NAND (NOT-AND) logic; NOR (NOT-OR) logic

Online public access libraries (OPACs), 90
Online resources
 catalogs, 117–20, 120tab
 commercial online publications, 109
 libraries, online, 89–95
OPACs (online public access libraries), 90
OpenText, 129tab
Opposite outcomes (inversions), 10
OR logic
 AND logic, comparison, 51
 for circuit, parallel, 47fig, 47–48
 decision making, combining AND logic, 67–71, 74
 defined, 43–45
 for keyword (root word) searches, 55
 for partial-word (truncation) searches, 55, 76–77
 pipe (|) for, 50, 63
 searching databases with, 50–51
 for synonyms, searching with, 53
 syntax of search engines and, 50
 truth tables for, 44tab, 45tab, 47tab
OR/AND/AND logic, 69, 69fig
OR/OR/AND logic, 69, 69fig, 70, 70fig
OR/OR/AND/AND logic, 71, 71fig
OR/OR/OR/AND logic, 68, 68fig, 71, 71fig
Outcome. *See also* AND logic; Conditions; If-Then logic; NAND (NOT-AND) logic; NOR (NOT-OR) logic; NOT logic; OR logic
 defined, 2, 5
 inversions (opposite outcomes), 10
 negative, 10
 number of conditions, effect on, 18, 45
 positive, 10
 prerequisite conditions for, 5

Partial-word searches, 55, 76–77
Pathfinder site, 109
Patterns of logic, 1–2
People Find Service (Lycos), 81–82
People Search (Yahoo!), 82
Person information system. *See also* Place
    information system; Searching tips;
    Thing information system
  address books, 82
  age-appropriate material, 84
  *caveat emptor* (searcher beware), 81, 85–86
  defined, 79, 81
  email addresses sources, 82
  email conferences, 83
  listservs (mailing lists), 83, 85–86
  newsfeed to newsgroups, 83
  newsgroups, 83–85
  postal addresses, telephone numbers,
      81–82
  Standard Industrial Classifications
      (SICs), 82
  vCard for contact information, 82
  white-pages sources, 81–82
  yellow-pages sources, 82–83
Personal computers, 76
Personal Newsfeeds, 129tab
Phone Number database (Lycos), 82
Phrase searches, 30
Pipe searches, 32
Place information system. *See also* Librar-
    ies; Person information system;
    Searching tips; Thing information
    system
  age-appropriate material, 88, 90, 96, 97
  books and resources for K-12, 90, 96, 97
  bookstores, 96–99
  defined, 79, 87
  search strategy for, 88–89
Plus sign (+) for AND logic, 30
Positive conditions, 8, 10, 15–20
Positive outcome, 10
Postal addresses sources, 81–82
Prerequisites for outcome, 5. *See also*
    Conditions
Printing information, 130
Professionally reviewed Internet sites, 110
Programming, 1
Public Library of Nashville and Davidson
    County (Tennessee), 94–95

Quality of information, 88, 108, 130
Question to clarify target, 25, 78
Quotation marks (" ") for phrase searches, 30

Rating/review sites, 110–11, 116, 116tab
Research time, saving, 27–28
Retrieve It! (MVP Solutions), 77
Robot systems, 110, 120–29, 129tab
Root word (keyword) searches, 55
Rules for search systems, 30, 32, 50, 63–64

Safe sites, 110. *See also* Age-appropriate
    searching
School cataloging software, 100–2
Search engines, defined, 110
Search Guard (Lycos), 117
Search software vendors, 89
Searcher beware *(caveat emptor)*, 79, 81,
    85–86, 108
Searching tips. *See also* Age-appropriate
    searching; Boolean logic; Decision
    making; Person information system;
    Place information system; Thing in-
    formation system
  ampersand (&) for AND logic, 30
  for AND logic, 25, 27–28, 30, 32, 51, 77
  asterisk (*) for partial-word searches, 55
  automated search routines, 110, 120–29,
      129tab
  case-sensitivity and, 63
  *caveat emptor* (searcher beware), 79, 81,
      85–86, 108
  on computer networks (Internet), 77
  data structures, 78
  excluding material, 25, 27–28, 40, 63
  expanding searches, 51, 55
  file-content searches, 77
  "find" command for, 76–77
  focus to find concept, 27–28
  how to hunt, 78–79
  information system selection and, 79
  for keyword (root word), OR logic, 55
  on local area network computers (intra-
      nets), 77
  for NAND (NOT-AND) logic, 40, 40fig
  narrowing searches, 25, 27–28, 32, 40, 51, 59
  for NOR (NOT-OR) logic, 58–59
  for OR logic, 50–51, 53, 55, 76–77
  for partial-word (truncation), OR logic,
      55, 76–77
  on personal computers, 76

for phrase searches, 30
pipe (|) for OR logic, 50, 63
pipe searches, 32
plus sign (+) for AND logic, 30
quality of information and, 88, 108, 130
question/statement to clarify target, 25, 78
quotation marks (" ") for phrase searches, 30
reasons for, 76
strategy, 78–79
string phrase for excluding material, 63
for synonyms, OR logic, 53
syntax (rules) for, 30, 32, 50, 63–64
telecommunication system speed, 77–78
for templates, 63
thinking complex and, 75
what to hunt, 78
when to hunt, 77–78
where to hunt, 76–77
who hunts, 76
why hunt, 76
Sequence (order) of conditions, 12
Sharing information, 130–31
SICs (Standard Industrial Classifications), 82
Spiders, 120–29, 129tab
Standard Industrial Classifications (SICs), 82
Statement to clarify target, 25, 78
Storage of information, 129–31
String phrase for excluding material, 63
Study Web, 120tab
Subject catalogs, 120tab
Switch-on/off logic patterns, 1, 22fig, 22–23, 23fig
Synonyms, searching with, 53
Syntax for search systems, 30, 32, 50, 63–64

Telecommunication system speed, 77–78
Telephone numbers sources, 81–82
Telnet application, 89, 104
Templates for searching, 63
Thing information system. *See also* Person information system; Place information system; Searching tips
age-appropriate material, 108, 110–11, 114–16, 117
automated search routines, 129, 129tab
blocking software, 110–11, 116, 120

catalogs, by subject headings, 117–18
*caveat emptor* (searcher beware), 108
commercial online publications, 109
by concept, 120
defined, 79, 107
electronic data storage, 107–8
family sites, 111–15
filtering software, 110–11, 116, 120
in folders, electronic, 130
full-text publications, 109
by keyword, 120
online catalogs, 117–20, 120tab
personal ideas, 130–31
printing, 130
professionally reviewed Internet sites, 110
quality of, 108, 130
rating/review sites, 110–11, 116, 116tab
robot systems, 110, 120–29
safe sites, 110
sharing information, 130–31
storage of information, 129–31
uniform resource locator (URL), 130
virtual world problems, 107–9
word processors and, 130
Thinking complex and knowledge, 75
Time-Warner's Pathfinder site, 109
Top 5% (Lycos), 116tab
Truncation searches, 55, 76–77
Truth tables
for AND logic, 15tab, 16tab, 17tab
for NAND (NOT-AND) logic, 36tab
for NOR (NOT-OR) logic, 58tab
for OR logic, 44tab, 45tab, 47tab

Uniform resource locator (URL), 130
Universal Decimal Classification, 120tab

vCard for contact information, 82
Virtual Tourist World Map, 120tab
Virtual world problems, 107–9

W3C Virtual Library, 116tab
Wanderers, 120–28
Webcat site, 90
WebCrawler, 129tab
WebCrawler Select, 116tab
White Pages (Lycos), 81–82
White-pages information sources, 81–82
Wilbur (RedTree Development Inc.), 77

Word processors, 130
World Wide Web. *See also* Internet; Searching tips
　libraries versus Web pages, 88–89
　problems with, 107–9
　Web browsers, 104

Yahoo!
　for blocking and filtering software vendors, 110

Internet Life, 116tab
People Search, 82
for search software vendors, 89
searching with, 117, 118–19, 120
Yahooligans, 117, 120tab
Yanoff's Internet Services List, 120tab
Yellow-pages information sources, 82–83

# About the Authors

Robert S. Houghton, Ph.D., is currently Co-Director of the Instructional Technology Specialist program and an assistant professor in the College of Education and Allied Professions at Western Carolina University, Cullowhee, North Carolina. In addition to scouting adventures with his three sons, Bob enjoys whitewater canoeing, trout fishing, hiking, and camping with his family in the surrounding Appalachian Mountains. His indoor interests include Webmaster projects that create courses and link communities and school curriculum into larger webs of learning (http://www.ceap.wcu.edu/houghton/home.html). Current online projects include CROP (Communities Resolving Our Problems), LAMP (Living American Memory Project), and ECO (Environmental Creative Organizers).

Janaye Matteson Houghton is a certified speech-language pathologist and Preschool Coordinator for children with disabilities at Jackson County Schools in Sylva, North Carolina. She is adjunct faculty at Western Carolina University in Cullowhee, North Carolina. Janaye received her Bachelor of Arts degree from Augustana College, Illinois, and her Master of Science degree from Eastern Illinois University. She has had two curriculum books published in that field: *Action Language Lessons* with coauthors Koenen and Kaler (Whitehaven Publishing, 1981) and *Homespun Language* (Whitehaven Publishing, 1982). She is coauthor with husband Robert Houghton of *Circuit Sense* (Teacher Ideas Press, 1994). Her writing about Boolean logic is based on her interest in the use and meaning of language.

*from* **Libraries Unlimited**

## THE INTERNET AND INSTRUCTION: Activities and Ideas, 2d Edition
*Ann E. Barron and Karen S. Ivers*

Technology in the classroom? It's easy! Designed for educators and students, this guide to telecommunications and the Internet demystifies the technology and provides relevant and easy-to-implement ideas and activities. Expanded coverage of Web resources and cross-curricular activities have been added to this new edition. **Grades 4–12.**
*xi, 244p. 8½x11 paper ISBN 1-56308-613-1*

## THE INTERNET RESOURCE DIRECTORY FOR K–12 TEACHERS AND LIBRARIANS, 98/99 Edition
*Elizabeth B. Miller*

This award-winning annual offers you access to current, accurate, useful information about the Internet. Designed for educators, it organizes material by curriculum areas. Sites are annotated and screened, and this edition has increased emphasis on sites with lesson plans. FREE URL ADDRESS UPDATES listed at www.lu.com. **Grades K–12.**
*xxii, 403p. 7x10 paper ISBN 1-56308-718-9*

## MULTIMEDIA PROJECTS IN EDUCATION: Designing, Producing, and Assessing
*Karen S. Ivers and Ann E. Barron*

Learn how to design, produce, and assess multimedia projects in the classroom with the "Decide, Design, Develop, and Evaluate" (DDDE) model introduced here. **Easy** to follow; **easy** to use! **Grades 4–12.**
*xviii, 201p. 8½x11 paper ISBN 1-56308-572-0*

## HYPERMEDIA AS A STUDENT TOOL: A Guide for Teachers, 2d Edition
*Marianne G. Handler and Ann S. Dana*

Help students become expert hypermedia authors and designers while they learn in subject areas across the curriculum! The authors show you how a variety of hypermedia programs operate, provide instructional strategies, and describe how you can create learning environments that encourage student collaboration. **Grades 3–12.**
*xxiv, 345p. 8½x11 paper ISBN 1-56308-569-0*

## COOPERATIVE LEARNING ACTIVITIES IN THE LIBRARY MEDIA CENTER, 2d Edition
*Lesley S. J. Farmer*

This revised edition of Farmer's popular work helps you understand, develop, and implement cooperative learning activities with middle and high school students. In each content area, look for new activities and detailed lesson plans, many technology based. **Grades 6–12.**
*ca. 260p. 8½x11 paper ISBN 1-56308-542-9*

**For a FREE catalog or to place an order, please contact:**

## Libraries Unlimited, Inc.
**Dept. B991 · P.O. Box 6633 · Englewood, CO 80155-6633**
**1-800-237-6124, ext. 1 · Fax: 303-220-8843 · E-mail: lu-books@lu.com**

**Check out our Web site!**
**www.lu.com**